Using your
Computer
The **beginner's** guide

Published by: Haynes Publishing
Sparkford, Yeovil, Somerset BA22 7JJ
Tel: 01963 442030 Fax: 01963 440001
Int. tel: +44 1963 442030 Fax: +44 1963 440001
E-mail: sales@haynes-manuals.co.uk
Web site: www.haynes.co.uk

British Library Cataloguing in Publication Data:
A catalogue record for this book is available from the British Library

ISBN 1 85960 972 4

Printed in Britain by J. H. Haynes & Co. Ltd, Sparkford

Throughout this book, trademarked names are used. Rather than put a
trademark symbol after every occurrence of a trademarked name, we use
the names in an editorial fashion only, and to the benefit of the trademark
owner, with no intention of infringement of the trademark. Where such
designations appear in this book, they have been printed with initial caps.

Whilst we at J. H. Haynes & Co. Ltd strive to ensure the accuracy and
completeness of the information in this manual, it is provided entirely at the
risk of the user. Neither the company nor the author can accept liability for
any errors, omissions or damage resulting therefrom. In particular, users
should be aware that component and accessory manufacturers, and
software providers, can change specifications without notice, thus
appropriate professional advice should always be sought.

Using your Computer

The beginner's guide

Kyle MacRae

Contents

Introduction

So you've finally taken the plunge and bought yourself a PC – or perhaps had one foisted upon you by an impatient offspring? Well, congratulations! May we say that you couldn't have picked a better time for it. Relatively speaking, today's personal computer is cheaper, smarter and vastly more powerful than those of yesteryear … but that's all by the by. What matters more in the present context is that it's much easier to get to grips with a computer than ever before.

It's getting better all the time.

For all its many marvels, the average personal computer has long been over-complicated, counter-intuitive and prone to doing the dumbest things at times. However, the introduction of Windows XP Home Edition, an operating system developed by Microsoft for domestic PCs, has gone a long way towards bridging the gap between a computer's capability and its usability. More often than not, you will discover that your PC will 'just work' – and that's a remarkable step forward in computer evolution.

The real keys to understanding your new machine are taking things slowly and keeping it simple. This is why you won't find us pointing out ten different ways to do everything. Rather, we'll concentrate exclusively on the absolute essentials and tackle each new subject in jargon-free plain English.

In time, you will doubtless want to learn more about your computer and what it can do for you. We would certainly encourage this: invoke the help of friends or colleagues, undertake a course in computing, or just spend a little time experimenting. But our present aim, while modest, is giving you the know-how you need to begin using your computer.

We will assume from the outset that you know next to, or absolutely, nothing about computers. Much of what follows will therefore appear trivial to those with some practical experience under their belts. But they can look elsewhere. This is unashamedly a manual for the complete beginner.

A personal note

I once worked as a computer consultant, helping newcomers to buy, set up and use their first PC. One afternoon, I found myself plugging together a client's brand new state-of-the-art computer system – an exuberant and ill-advised (though not by me) purchase which had set him back some ludicrous sum. When all was ready, I handed over the reins – well, the mouse – and proclaimed: 'OK, click the Start button and let's get going!'

Some 40 minutes later (I kid you not), we were still sat at that desk, trying repeatedly, desperately but ultimately unsuccessfully to make that click. For the avoidance of doubt, this client was a retired professional with dextrous hands, perfectly good eyesight and the full complement of faculties. But he just could not relate the movements of a slithery lump of plastic on a rubber mat to those of a pointer on his PC's monitor screen. I shared his frustration as the pointer darted around the screen from corner to corner, beyond his control and beyond his ken; and I may even have echoed his soft curse when finally the pointer came close enough to the Start button to hazard a speculative click … only for the mouse to wobble in his hand and send the pointer skating across the screen once more.

It struck me then, as it strikes me now, that there is a pressing need for a practical guide that makes no assumptions whatsoever about the relationship between a computer and its owner. A mouse is not an intuitive way to control a computer, any more than pressing a pedal is an intuitive way to make a car go faster, or stop; these things have to be taught, learned and practised, not taken for granted and glossed over.

This, then, is the book written for the frustrated 'newbie' who really wants to use a computer but isn't quite sure where to start … and doesn't fancy taking a degree in geekology just to be able to send an e-mail.

How to use this book

For the sake of consistency and clarity, we will use certain conventions throughout this manual.

Mouse instructions

When you see the 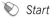 symbol, we are referring to an action performed with the mouse. So, for instance,

 Start

means 'use the mouse to move the on-screen pointer to the Start button, and click it'.

Furthermore, most mouse-driven actions involve several steps. Each step starts on a new line. As a rule, when we say 'click', we mean click the left mouse button once.
Don't worry – this will become clear soon enough.

There are two other mouse actions, double click and right button click. All three actions appear as follows;

 Single click on the left mouse button

 Double click on the left mouse button

Single click on the right mouse button

Screen examples

Mouse instructions

Keyboard instructions

Text instructions

4

New Folder icon

Rename this folder

Home Finances [Enter]

This step only applies if Step 3 goes wrong and you didn't manage to rename the folder while 'New Folder' was highlighted. Select New Folder by clicking its icon once. Now look in the left window pane and you'll see an option to Rename this folder. Click this and once again the folder's title becomes highlighted. Now just type in the new name and press the Enter key. Any folder can be renamed in this manner.

5

Home Finances icon

Make a new folder

Bank Correspondence [Enter]

Following the example discussed above, we now want to create a sub-folder within Home Finances called Bank Correspondence. Double-click the Home Finances folder icon to open the folder (which is, of course, currently empty). Now create and name a new folder just as in 2 and 3 above. Once again, you can easily in Step 4 if anything goes wrong.

Keyboard instructions

When you see the symbol, the directions refer to the keyboard. For example:

 teapot

means 'type the word "teapot" on the keyboard now'. Type exactly what you see, being sure to note any spaces or unusual symbols.

However, when the direction is contained within square brackets, this indicates that you should type something that pertains to you specifically e.g.

 [your e-mail address]

means 'type in your own e-mail address'. We'll soon have you using the keyboard with abandon.

When we want you to press a certain key on the keyboard, this is denoted by means of a box. Thus

 [Enter]

means 'press the Enter key'.

Where an action requires you to press more than one key simultaneously, we use the + symbol to link them. Thus

 [Ctrl] + [Alt] + [Delete]

is an instruction to press the three named keys at the same time. And it really doesn't get any more complicated than that!

Text instructions

Beneath the mouse and keyboard directions, we explain the purpose and method of each step in more detail. Please read these instructions in full before clicking the mouse or typing on the keyboard.

Jargon

Any word or phrase highlighted like *this* is fully explained in the glossary. This helps to keep the main text clear of non-essential clutter. To avoid an over-complicated appearance, we only highlight the first occurrence of the word or phrase.

Screen examples

We also make frequent use of 'screenshots' to illustrate the effect of a given procedure. However, it is not always possible to show every single step along the way so be sure to follow the mouse, keyboard and text instructions carefully.

PART # From delivery to desktop

Let's assume that you've just taken delivery of several rather large and heavy panic-inducing boxes. If you had just bought a television set or some hi-fi equipment, you could be reasonably confident of connecting a couple of cables, plugging it into the mains electricity and being able to sit back and enjoy the fruit of your labours. But this is a computer system, and you just *know* that it's going to stress you out.

Perhaps you've already called your colleagues, neighbours or the emergency services for assistance. But relax. In just a few pages time, you'll be using your PC for the very first time. We're going to talk you through unpacking and setting up your shiny new computer system so that it works first time around ... and keeps on working.

PART ① A (very) potted guide to PCs

Be honest, now – how much do you really want to know about your computer? You don't have to grasp the workings of an internal combustion engine to drive a car or comprehend the mysteries of twisted-pair copper wiring to pick up the telephone. Most computer manuals (in our admittedly biased opinion) go into far too much detail, leaving you a good deal more knowledgeable but not necessarily better equipped to do something useful like writing a letter. So here instead is a brief look at the basics. We'll get through it as quickly as we possibly can.

Your computer system is essentially composed of two parts, hardware and software.

Hardware

First, let's consider the nuts and bolts.

The system unit Or, if you prefer, the case. System units are usually tall, thin 'tower' affairs these days but you can still buy squat, wide cases called, confusingly, 'desktop' PCs. There is no practical difference between the two aside from the design; a desktop PC is basically a tower case on its side. See illustration below.

The system unit has two important buttons on the front: an on/off switch, and a reset switch. The first controls the power supply to the computer, and the second is used to *restart* the computer if it ever 'hangs' i.e. freezes in the middle of an operation. Windows XP has largely made this hassle a thing of the past.

Inside the system unit is a large printed circuit board known as the motherboard, or mainboard. This hosts the *processor* and *memory* and all the other electronic gubbins that make a computer smart. Everything that plays a part in your computer system connects to the *motherboard* in one way or another.

Floppy disc drive

CD drive

DVD-ROM drive

Reset switch

On/off switch

System unit

Monitor

Speakers

Keyboard

Mouse

Peripherals

If the system unit is the PC proper, everything else can be called a peripheral device. But what does it all do?

Monitor A display screen on which you view images generated by your computer.

Keyboard A typewriter-like input device. Every press of a key generates a signal that the computer interprets and acts upon. Basically, it's one way of feeding instructions to your computer.

Mouse This handheld input device controls a pointer on the monitor screen. By pointing at on-screen objects and clicking the mouse's buttons, you make your computer do stuff. This is the other way of feeding instructions to your computer.

Speakers Without speakers, your computer can emit only the odd forlorn bleep. With speakers, it rocks.

Printer A device that turns computer-generated content into paper documents. Thus you might write a letter or draw a picture on your computer and print out a hard copy on your printer. Inkjet printers print in colour and are ideal for family use; laser printers generally print in black and white only but achieve a higher quality suitable for professional stationery.

Scanner A device that takes a photograph of anything you place under the lid, turns it into an electronic image and sends it to your computer. Ideal for scanning snapshots or documents.

Forget the dream of a 'paperless world' – printers still have a place.

Although an optional extra, a scanner is useful for turning paper-based documents and images into computer files.

Drives

A drive is a device that reads *data* from and, sometimes, writes data to magnetic or optical media. In plain English, drives let you access and save information.

Hard disk drive At the heart of any PC is the hard *disk* drive. This is where files you create are saved. It is also home to the computer's operating system and application software, more of which shortly. Without a hard disk drive, your PC would be an empty shell with no memory and about as useful as a mobile phone on Mars. The hard disk drive is hidden away inside the case.

Floppy disk drive This drive uses cheap but low-capacity magnetic disks called, rather misleadingly, floppies.

CD drive A CD drive can do one or more of these: read data from a pre-recorded compact *disc* (*CD-ROM*); save data onto a blank compact disc, but just once (*CD-R*); and save data onto a compact disc time and time again, overwriting existing data as required (*CD-RW*). A CD-RW drive, as shown here, can actually do all three.

DVD-ROM drive Now virtually standard equipment on new computers. DVD discs have a far greater capacity than CDs, which makes them ideal for distributing huge volumes of data. Your DVD drive can also play *DVD movies*. However, you cannot save your own data onto DVD discs. For that, you'd need a special recordable DVD drive. These are still rather heavily priced and considered more of a luxury than an essential. Your PC may have a CD/DVD 'combo' drive that combines CD and DVD functions within a single unit.

Power supply

Power switch

MESH MATRIX XP
4868333-001-s

Mouse socket

Keyboard socket

USB ports

Serial port

Parallel port

More USB ports

Audio inputs and outputs

Even more USB ports

Monitor socket

MONITOR

Phone line socket

Modem

FAX/MODEM

Sound card

Games socket

Windows XP
Home Edition.

Interfaces

It's time to look around the back. Scary stuff? Not a bit of it. First off, near the top, you'll find a large three-pin socket for connecting the power supply and possibly a power switch. Once you've connected the power cable and flicked the power switch to the on position, you shouldn't need to bother with these again.

Just about everything else is an *interface* of some sort – that is, a port or socket used to connect other hardware devices to the system unit. In fact, there are two types of interfaces: integrated and expansion cards. Okay, this is getting just a little jargony but bear with us for a moment.

Integrated interfaces are permanently soldered to the motherboard. In this example, we see sockets for the mouse and keyboard, four *USB* ports, two *serial* ports one *parallel* port, and a bunch of audio inputs and outputs. Your computer might also have an *Ethernet* port if it has been designed to connect to other computers in a *network*.

Lower down the case, we find several other input and output interfaces grouped together in rows. These are expansion cards. An expansion card is simply a circuit board that plugs in to the internal motherboard. Each is dedicated to a particular function or range of related duties. The main attraction of expansion cards is that they can be easily removed and replaced, which adds flexibility and expansion possibilities to your PC.

Topmost is yet another pair of USB ports. Below these we find the *video card*. This expansion card is responsible for producing the pictures you see on your monitor screen. The monitor plugs in here.

The next two slots are currently covered by metal 'blanking plates' but these could be easily removed from within if we wanted to install new expansion cards.

Below them is the *modem*, essential for connecting your computer to the internet. One socket is used to connect the modem to the telephone line; the other lets you connect a telephone handset.

The next expansion card is the *sound card*, to which you connect speakers and, optionally, headphones, a microphone or pretty much any external sound source. The sound card, you see, is just as well equipped to record sound as it is to play music and make other noises.

Finally, we find a games socket, used to connect a joystick or other controller when playing computer games. You could also connect a *MIDI* instrument here to record your own music. The games socket is usually found on the sound card itself but in this case there simply wasn't room and so it has been given a slot all of its own.

Software

Software is any set of coded instructions that a computer can understand. When you press a key on the keyboard, the computer knows that something has happened; however, it takes software to turn the raw electronic signal into an instruction to display, say, the letter Q. We'll look at software in detail later but for now let's concentrate on an absolutely critical trichotomy that baffles even many experienced computer owners: the difference between the operating system, application software and driver software.

Operating system A multi-faceted software program that runs the computer. In the present case, this is a program developed by Microsoft called Windows XP Home Edition. Windows is a graphical program, which means you interact with it by means of on-screen objects and *menus* i.e. you don't have to learn a complex language of text commands. This makes computers easy to use. It does not, however, make them entirely intuitive, which is why we've written this manual.

From now on, we will refer to the operating system simply as Windows.

Application software Although an operating system like Windows contains many useful programs that go well beyond the basics of running the computer, it is not by itself sufficient to make a PC practical in the long term. For this you need application software i.e. dedicated programs designed for specific tasks. You need application software to write a letter, surf the internet or play around with *digital* pictures.

From now on, we will refer to application software simply as programs.

Driver software Special code that enables a computer to interact with hardware devices. When you buy, for instance, a new scanner, you will find two types of software in the box: application software, with which to edit scanned images, but also – and more importantly – driver software. The driver tells the computer that a scanner has just been bolted on to the system, that it's this particular make and model of scanner, and that it's capable of doing X, Y and Z. Without a driver sitting between the device and the operating system, nothing happens.

From now on, we will refer to the driver software simply as drivers.

All clear? Windows runs your computer, programs let you do interesting things with it, and drivers make your hardware work.

PART

Preparing your workstation

Your very first task before unpacking a thing should be deciding where to put it all. Computer equipment is heavy, fragile and a pain to shift from here to there, so let's plan it properly from the outset. We'll assume here that your computer system comprises a system unit, monitor, keyboard, mouse, speakers, printer and scanner. That's pretty much the norm these days.

Workstation or desk?

Workstations come in many shapes and sizes, from corner-hugging, space-saving, vertically-stacking units to great, sprawling, semi-permanent installations. The choice is yours, but we would caution against underestimating how much room your computer needs. Even with everything tucked away, you'll still need sufficient space to site your keyboard directly in front of the monitor with a mouse mat alongside. What about the speakers? The printer and scanner? A telephone? Will you still be able to lay out documents as you work on them? Factor in a little personal elbow room, too: you will, after all, spend a good deal of time with your computer (no, really, you will).

The main attraction of a purpose-built workstation is that you can find one to fit any available space. But don't be tempted to splash out if you have a perfectly serviceable desk to hand.

Support your wrists with a gel-filled rest.

Power points

Your computer system is going to require five plug sockets: one each for the system unit, monitor, speakers, printer and scanner. We would also suggest that you invest in a desk lamp, which makes it six. Invest in one or two of those power strip extensions with multiple sockets, and check that they comfortably extend to the rear of your workstation or desk. Moreover, only buy power strips with 'surge protection' built in. This will protect your valuable equipment if the electricity supply is subject to any fluctuations, such as those caused by heavy electrical equipment on the same mains circuit.

You might also consider an 'uninterruptible power supply' (i.e. a battery-powered unit that sits between your computer and the mains power and temporarily takes over in the event of a power cut).

To use the internet, you will need access to a telephone socket. It might be worthwhile getting your telephone company to install a fresh socket behind your workstation, or perhaps installing an extension yourself. Failing that, plan how you will connect the back-end of your computer to the nearest socket. Trailing a cable across the carpet, under doors and up the stairs is not conducive to domestic harmony.

Also consider nearby sources of heat and light. Your computer will thank you not to be sited too close to a radiator, and you must allow it adequate ventilation (i.e. at least 30cm of clear space around the rear of the system unit and the monitor vents). Sit directly facing a window and you'll spend all summer squinting at the screen; sit with a window behind you and the screen will reflect the light back into your eyes. Your monitor generates its own bright images without the need for any external lighting so do your eyes a favour and avoid screen glare, even if it means compromising on the ideal site for your computer.

Are you sitting comfortably?

Ergonomics, or the study of workplace design, is more a case of common sense than hard science. When arranging your workstation, there are two main considerations: comfort and safety. By comfort, we mean that you shouldn't have to crick your neck to see the monitor, prop yourself up on cushions to use the keyboard or crawl under the desk to reach your computer's CD-ROM drive. By safety, however, we must consider the dangers of using a computer for prolonged periods. Chief amongst the hazards is Repetitive Strain Injury, or RSI, involving such unpleasant complaints as tenosynovitis, tendonitis and carpal tunnel syndrome. Regular breaks and stretching exercises are advisable during a long session at the desk but equally important is adopting a sensible posture. Above all, any discomfort is a sign of stress, so respect your body's signals and take action before it is too late. RSI is a debilitating and often agonising condition.

Invest in a fully-adjustable chair to save yourself from backache. A three-legged Chippendale copy liberated from the dining room really isn't up to the job.

Good posture and careful planning help avoid RSI.

Good posture begins with a straight back. A decent chair is essential but equally so is a cast-iron resolution not to hunch over your keyboard or slump in your seat.

When using the keyboard, your forearms should be horizontal and held at approximately 90° to your upper arms.

The back and the seat of your chair should both be adjustable for height and tilt. Adjustable arm rests are a good idea, and the chair should be absolutely stable. A five-legged platform is more stable than a three-legged one.

The top of your monitor screen should be no higher than eye level. Indeed, some research suggests that the monitor should ideally be positioned between 15° and 50° below eye level, much like you would hold a magazine. The screen should be at least 60cm away from your face.

Position the monitor directly in front of you, not offset to one side.

Your feet should be flat on the floor and your thighs horizontal or, preferably, tilted slightly forwards. Use a foot rest if necessary (no, not your scanner) to maintain a 90° angle between the thighs and shins. This helps support your back.

PART Plugging it all together

Here comes the daunting part – unpacking your new PC system and making it work. We'll assume that you've already sneaked a peep inside the boxes and panicked at the sight of endless CD-ROMs, manuals and cables. How on earth are you supposed to know where to start?

Get organised

First things first: let's unpack. Your computer system will be packed in several boxes, typically one each for the monitor, speakers, printer and scanner, and a further carton containing the system unit, keyboard, mouse and various bits and pieces. Carefully take everything out, lay it out on the floor and check it against the delivery paperwork. This may be easier said than done, of course – you may not appreciate (or particularly care) that 'ATI RADEON 8500 64MB DV (ALL IN WONDER)' refers to the computer's internal video card, so simply keep an eye open for obvious omissions. If there's no monitor, get on the blower.

Here is a list of everything delivered with our system:

- One computer in a tower system unit
- One **CRT** monitor with manual
- One keyboard
- One **5.1** speaker system with cables, power supply and set-up guide
- One large, clearly illustrated and very welcome installation sheet
- One printer
- One scanner

'It'll be nice when it's finished,' you muse hopefully when confronted with boxes of unconnected hardware. And you're right . . . it will be.

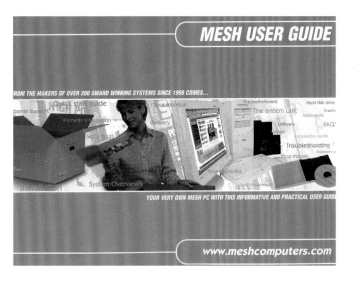

Well, you've already got this manual so you may not need the one that comes with your computer. But keep it safe just in case.

So far, so obvious. But then we came upon this little lot:

User guide The main manual! Very important.

Customer support guide Equally important. This tells you how to get technical help.

Two three-pin power cables One each for the system unit and the monitor.

Modem cable Connects the PC's modem to the phone socket.

Monitor adaptor This little adaptor means that we can connect our older-style CRT monitor to the *DVI* interface on the video card.

Video card manual You may need to refer to the manual to understand the video card's features.

Motherboard manual If you ever open up your computer to perform an upgrade, this manual will prove invaluable. Until then, keep it safe and don't give it another thought.

Modem manual This will come in useful later when we set up our internet connection.

Windows XP recovery CD-ROM This can get you out of trouble if your PC starts to experience severe problems.

Sound card CD-ROM This disc contains the drivers necessary to get the sound card working. However, most computer manufacturers pre-install essential software so that your computer works 'straight out of the box'. This disc would only be required if you ever had to re-install the sound card.

Video card CD-ROM Ditto.

Modem CD-ROM Ditto.

Video-editing CD-ROM Programs for editing video footage on the PC.

CD-burning CD-ROM Programs for recording data, audio or video compilations onto blank CDs.

Office suite CD-ROM Programs for writing letters, keeping records and doing all sorts of creative things like that. You may have been supplied with an armful of application software – or none at all.

Mouse mat A mat for the mouse.

Oh, and the mouse The mouse itself.

Phew! Little wonder people panic.

A monitor adaptor lets you connect an older-style CRT (big, bulky, cheap) monitor to a DVI video card designed for digital LCD (flat, lightweight, more expensive) monitors.

Laying it out

Set up the key components – system unit, monitor, keyboard and mouse – roughly as you plan to use them. Don't worry about the cables and wiring; everything can hang loose for now.

If you've bought an older-style CRT monitor, you will probably have to attach a swivel base to its underside first. This is usually straightforward, but start as you mean to go on and consult the monitor manual.

Now have a seat and see if it all feels just about right. Pay particular attention to any sources of glare on the monitor screen. Take the time now to make any adjustments, even if it means moving your workstation across the room or rethinking your power source. It's a good deal easier doing this now than after having made all the hardware connections.

Now bring the printer and scanner into play. Don't worry yet about any tape or security packing on these devices; simply take them from their boxes and make sure they fit their allotted space. In particular, remember that your printer will need to have input and output trays bolted on, which significantly increases its working area.

Finally, unpack and arrange your speakers. This could involve anywhere from two simple stereo speakers to four or five speakers if you opted for a 4.1 or 5.1 *'surround sound'* system. We'll assume the latter here.

Unpack the smaller satellite speakers, attach any stands supplied and note the length of their cables. You should find that two speakers (or three in a 5.1 system) come with relatively short cables, perhaps a couple of metres each. Two others will have longer cables, typically five metres. One speaker with a short cable should be positioned either side of the monitor, equidistant from your seated position but with as much space between them as possible. The third short-cabled speaker (5.1 system only) should be sited as centrally as possible, perhaps on a shelf above the monitor or indeed perched on the monitor itself. In truth, only a true audiophile would object if you tucked it in to one side of the monitor.

The speakers with longer cables should now be located either side of and behind your seated position for the full surround sound effect.

At this point it's quite possible that all the computer salesman's patter about DVD movie soundtracks stunningly rendered in surround sound Dolby Digital will pale into insignificance when you realise that, in fact, there's just no convenient way to locate these satellites in your living room. If so, now is the time to cut your losses and settle for simple stereo sound, in which case you don't need the rear or central satellites at all.

With or without rear speakers, you will certainly want to use a *subwoofer* if one was supplied. This is a large, powerful unit that broadcasts deep bass tones. It should be located at floor level but needn't be centrally positioned (i.e. you don't have to stick it between your feet).

Once more, with everything roughly in place, satisfy yourself with your workstation arrangement.

Arrange your hardware as you intend to use it before making connections.

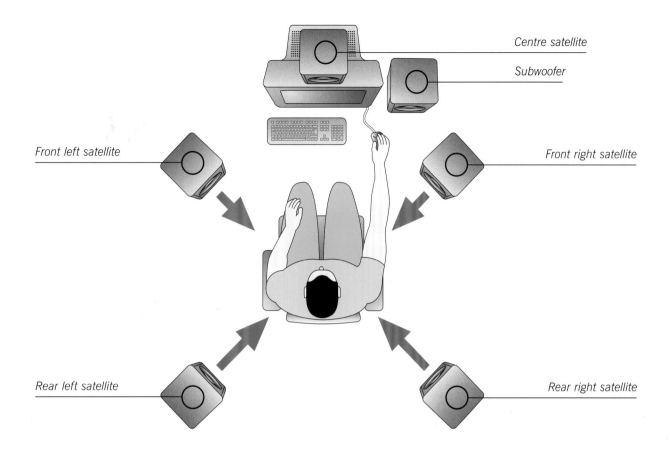

Centre satellite

Subwoofer

Front left satellite

Front right satellite

Rear left satellite

Rear right satellite

A 5.1 surround sound system requires careful speaker placement.

Making connections

It's time to turn all this raw hardware into a working computer.

As we have already seen, the rear of the system unit hosts a range of electronic interfaces, each of which lets you connect a device to the system. Right now, you need to identify four, namely:

Monitor. This is either a blue *analogue* socket (*VGA*) for use with older-style CRT monitors or a white digital socket (DVI) for use with digital *LCD* monitors.

Just to confuse the issue, here we have to connect a CRT monitor to a DVI socket, hence the presence of the adaptor plug we unearthed earlier. In most cases, however, the thick white cable hard-wired to the monitor plugs straight into a VGA or DVI socket.

Keyboard. A round socket, usually colour-coded purple. The connector on the keyboard's cable is coloured correspondingly. How handy is that?

Mouse. A similar story to the keyboard, but in green.

Speakers. Not so simple. Take a deep breath …

In our example, the PC has two sets of 3.5mm audio connectors. This is because the manufacturer has disabled the motherboard's integrated sound system in favour of a superior sound card. Now, your particular system may have either integrated sound or a sound card, in which case there is no choice and little room for confusion. But it may have both, as here, and only the sound card will do the business. So how do you identify which is which?

Easy. Integrated connectors are always found in close proximity to the keyboard and mouse sockets whereas the sound card's connectors are located within the array of expansion card slots. Flick back to the potted guide on page 14 if you're in any doubt.

In a surround sound system, the speakers do not actually connect to the sound card directly; rather, they are connected to the subwoofer, which itself connects to the sound card.

Inevitably, all this plugging together of speakers involves a good deal of crawling around at floor level, which is why once again we urge you to be sure that you're happy with your workstation before you make a start.

When you have identified these essentials, you can start to hook it all together.

Fancy speakers require fancy connections. Here, the five satellite speakers all plug into the subwoofer, and then the subwoofer hooks up to the system unit.

Begin with the monitor. Note how the shaped connector on the monitor cable fits the PC's socket in only one direction. Line them up and gently push the connector home, taking great care not to force it or bend the pins. Now secure the cable in position with the connector's integrated screws. Do NOT over-tighten them – the idea is merely to ensure that the connector will not slip or be easily knocked out of its socket. In this case, we are using the adaptor described above.

Now connect the keyboard and mouse. Note again that the pins on the connector and the holes in the socket must be carefully aligned. Follow the colour coding or look for descriptive stickers on the case next to the sockets. Place the keyboard directly in front of the monitor on your desktop and the mouse on its mat to either the right or the left depending upon whether you're right- or left-handed.

3 *The precise method for wiring up the speaker system depends upon your equipment but you will have been supplied with a guide. In this case, we have five satellite speakers to connect to the subwoofer. The subwoofer then connects to the sound card by means of three 3.5mm audio jacks. Take the time to ensure that each speaker is connected to the correct channel on the subwoofer (e.g. the speaker that sits to the left of the monitor on your workstation should be connected to the channel marked 'front left').*

4 *Connect the three-pin power cables to the system unit and monitor and plug them into the power strip. If the PC's power supply unit has a voltage selector, take a second to check that it is set correctly for your country (e.g. 240V in the UK). The PC's power supply unit may also have an on-off switch; if so, flick it to the on position now. Also plug the subwoofer into the power strip. Look for a power switch or button on the subwoofer case and turn it on. Volume controls should be set about a third of the way between minimum and maximum.*

And that's that. Just to refresh:

- The monitor should be connected to the system unit's video card.
- The keyboard and mouse should be connected to the system unit.
- The satellite speakers should be connected to the subwoofer.
- The subwoofer should be connected to the system unit's sound card.
- The system unit, monitor and subwoofer should all be plugged into a surge-protected power strip.

Now plug the power strip into the mains electricity and flick the switch. Ready for some action? Turn to the next section.

PART

Turning on for the first time ... and off again

Caller: 'Hello, technical support? I need help! My computer won't work properly.'

Technical Support: 'Hmm. Have you tried booting it?'

Caller: 'Hold on ...'

A sickening crunch is heard

Caller: 'No, that didn't seem to help.'

Boot camp

To 'boot' (or 'power-up') a computer is to switch it on, so let's do just that. Shuffle your computer system back into the right arrangement on your workstation – everything may have moved about when you made the connections – and take a seat at your workstation.

It's good practice to turn on the monitor first because it means you can read any messages that appear on screen. Do this now. There's usually a biggish button on the front, but check the manual if you're not certain.

Now push the larger button on the front of the system unit. Hear that whirring sound? That's the internal cooling fans springing into action, without which your computer would melt. Watch the screen and you'll likely see some gobbledegook in white letters on a black background. That's fine; ignore it. Soon, you will see a Windows welcome screen followed quickly by the Windows Desktop. You will even hear a congratulatory tune tinkle forth from your speakers. This is Windows saying hello.

Exactly what you see at this point depends upon how your computer manufacturer has set up your system, but as long as there's a green button labelled 'start' in the lower left corner of the screen – hereafter referred to as the Start *button* – you've made it. This is the Desktop. Windows XP is up and running and ready for action.

The great escape

Here's an oddity: the very first thing you should do having turned on your computer is turn it straight back off again. This is because it is very, very important to learn the correct approach and follow it every time. Here's another oddity: switching off begins with the Start button.

We're going to practise using the mouse shortly, so for now you may not find the following steps natural or easy. But just take your time and you'll get there (well, hopefully – now might be a good time to forget all about that client mentioned in the introduction).

Your first encounter with Windows Desktop and that all-important Start button.

QUICK Q & A

How do I change my Desktop picture to something more interesting?

- Start
- Control Panel
- Appearance and Themes icon
- Change the Desktop background
- Browse.

Now navigate to any picture file saved on your hard disk (probably to be found in the My Pictures folder within My Documents). If you want to use a picture of your own, save it with either a .bmp or .jpeg extension first.

QUICK Q & A

Why does my monitor/hard disk keep turning itself off after a couple of hours?

This is all to do with power-saving settings. Computers are designed to run all day and night but you can save on the electricity bills by having them click into standby mode at times of inactivity. The settings can be accessed and changed here:

 Start

 Control Panel

 Performance and Maintenance icon

 Power Options

---

①

 Start

When you move the mouse around on its mat, the onscreen pointer matches its movements. Push the mouse forwards (i.e. towards the back of your desk) and the pointer moves up the screen; slide it to the right and the pointer follows suit. Your task is to make the pointer point at the Start button in the lower left corner of the screen. When it's in position, press and release the left mouse button with your index finger. This is called clicking. If the mouse jerks out of position at this point, just use your other hand to keep it steady and persevere. Don't worry, this will all become second-nature soon enough!

②

 Turn Off Computer

When you make a successful 'click', a menu will pop up above the Start button. Right at the bottom, you'll see a red button labelled Turn Off Computer. Move the mouse until the pointer points straight at this button, and click it once again.

③

 Turn Off Computer

Up pops a box with three buttons: Stand By, Turn Off and Restart. This time, make the pointer point at the middle button, Turn Off, and click the left mouse button again. Windows will now shut itself down. It may also switch off the system unit and perhaps even the monitor. If not, you'll see a message telling you that it's safe to turn off your computer. This is your cue to push the power switch on the system unit case to kill the power. Turn off the monitor, too.

PART 2 **First steps**

OK, so you've set up your computer and turned it on and off. Our guess is that you're itching to do something *useful* with it ... but we're going to crave your indulgence and ask you to hang fire a while longer. These next few pages are absolutely critical: if you can master mouse and keyboard control right from the outset, even at the most basic level, all that follows will be so much easier.

We'll also get your printer and scanner up and running in this section.

PART # Make friends with your mouse

A natural extension of your hand, or a slippery lump of plastic that slides around out of control and drives you to distraction? Like it or loathe it, the mouse is such an integral part of modern computing that nothing pays dividends like mastering it early.

Anatomy of a mouse

Windows is a graphical operating system for your computer, which means that you get to work with pictures and other visual clues instead of having to type text commands (as in the *bad old days*). The mouse enables you to interact with these graphics.

As in Part 1, you can see this by moving the mouse on its mat while Windows is running – every motion is replicated by the onscreen pointer.

Hardware-wise, the average modern mouse has two buttons with a wheel lodged between them. The left button is the primary button – i.e. it is used most frequently and performs most common tasks – while the right button generally invokes special shortcuts. The wheel, if present, can have a number of functions but is mainly used to 'scroll' through long documents and *web pages*.

Most mice have an integrated rubber ball on their undersides and work best on hard rubber mats that help the ball rotate freely and accurately.

Hold your mouse gently but firmly as shown below with your index and middle fingers resting lightly on the buttons. Practise just sliding it around the mat for a while and watch the onscreen pointer mimic its movements. It's very relaxing. Unfortunately, it doesn't get you very far.

The mouse pointer is an onscreen arrow controlled by your mouse. Use it to, er, point at things, and click them.

There's no need to squeeze the life out of your mouse – hold it gently, get your fingers in position and practise until it feels natural.

Keep your mouse free from fluff to keep it running smoothly.

Some funky things to do with a mouse

Here, then, are the key mouse concepts used in everyday home computing. Refer to the Conventions section on pages 8-9 for a refresher on the symbols used below.

Point-and-click. *This is where you make the onscreen pointer point at something, like an icon or a menu, and then press and release the left mouse button. It makes a satisfying clicking sound, hence the term 'click'. This is generally abbreviated to, for example, 'click the Start button'.*

 Start

 Start

Use the mouse to make the onscreen pointer point at the Start button in the bottom-left corner of your screen and click the left button once. This makes the Start Menu pop up. Now click the button again to make the menu disappear. What could be simpler?

Double-click. *Instead of pressing and releasing the mouse button once, here you click it twice in rapid succession. Why? Well, in certain circumstances, the first click merely 'selects' the given object and the second click 'activates' it. Unless we specifically say 'double-click', assume that any direction refers to a single-click.*

 Clock

 Cancel

OK, this takes some explaining! Your computer's clock is tucked away in the very bottom-right corner of your screen. Point at the digits and click the left mouse button twice quickly. Up pops a window with lots of nice clock options, including a way to change the time. We don't want to do this, however, so click the Cancel button – a single-click this time – to make the window go away.

Don't fret if you struggle with this one, particularly if the mouse moves slightly between clicks or you don't manage to click quickly enough to launch the clock. We'll show you a way to make life easier in a moment. When you can launch and close the clock window with impunity, award yourself a well-earned Double-click Diploma.

Right-click. *Simple enough: click the right mouse button instead of the left. Generally speaking, a right-click launches a shortcut menu pertaining to the task in hand. You could (just about) get by without ever right-clicking but Windows is designed with shortcuts in mind so we'll use right-click directions occasionally. Here's one to get you started.*

 Recycle Bin icon

 Properties

 Cancel

*This means right-click the Recycle Bin icon on the Desktop, then left-click the Properties entry on the **pop-up** shortcut menu, and finally left-click the Cancel button in the Recycle Bin Properties **dialogue box**.*

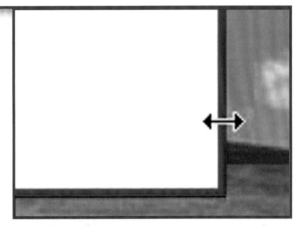

Drag. *Another absolutely central mouse operation. Dragging involves a click-and-hold manoeuvre whereby you point at something, press the left mouse button and then keep the button depressed instead of releasing it straight away.*

 My Computer icon

Double-click the My Computer icon on the Desktop. This opens a window that contains some useful information about your computer but we're only interested in the window itself for now. Move the onscreen pointer right to one edge of the window. See how it suddenly changes shape to a double-headed arrow? Your task now is to click and hold the left mouse button just as the pointer changes. Then, keeping the button depressed, move the double-headed arrow slightly to the left and slightly to the right. The window will expand and contract accordingly. When you release the mouse button, the window stays the way you leave it.

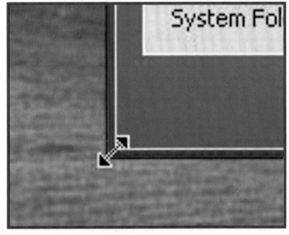

Now try the same technique with the top and bottom edge of the window and expand/contract it vertically.

Finally – and this is much trickier – point at one of the window's corners and watch the pointer change shape to a slanted double-headed arrow. Now click, hold and drag in a diagonal direction. This resizes the window horizontally and vertically simultaneously.

When you're finished, click the small cross in the top-right corner to close the My Computer window.

Drag-and-drop. *A closely related discipline that involves moving an object rather than resizing it. The initial technique is just the same.*

 My Computer icon

This time, point at the middle of the Title Bar (i.e. the wide, coloured upper-edge of the window that tells you the name of the window – in this case, My Computer). The pointer will not change shape. Now click the left mouse button and, keeping the button depressed as before, drag the entire window up, down and all around the Desktop. See how it follows the movements of the mouse? At any time, you can release the mouse button to 'drop' the window in a new position. Again, close the window when you've finished by clicking the small cross in the top-right corner.

Well, we're getting a little ahead of ourselves here, playing around with serious concepts like icons and windows before offering any real explanation as to what these things are and how they work. It's all a bit chicken and egg, really – it's important to be competent with the mouse and keyboard before tackling Windows but acquiring this competency inevitably involves using Windows. Still, not to worry. It is all good practice and will all make perfect sense soon enough.

Practice makes perfect

So much for the theory. But having already used the mouse to shut down your computer, you may be worried that you'll never get the hang of the thing. Here's an easy and fun way to practise. First, turn on your computer. Then do this:

 Start

 All Programs

 Games

 Solitaire

What we have here is Windows' own electronic version of the card game Solitaire, or Patience, and it's a great way to develop accurate mouse control. These directions obviously relate to one particular deal of the cards but just apply the general principles.

The Ace of any suit can be dragged to one of the vacant stacking areas above the main playing area. Here the Ace of Spades happens to be in column four. Point at the card, click and hold the left mouse button, then carefully drag the card to the leftmost stacking area. Now release the mouse button. Don't worry if you mess it up a few times, as the card will simply snap back to its original position on the 'table'.

3

To move the red Seven onto the black Eight (or whatever), click on the card and drag-and-drop it into position i.e. release the mouse button when it's positioned roughly over the Eight of Clubs. You don't have to be too precise. See how it automatically snaps into place? Move as many cards as you can at this point.

4

Now you need to flip over any newly-exposed cards. Point at each in turn and click once to turn it over. If this opens up new playing possibilities, drag and drop the cards as before. The Two of any suit may be dragged away from the main playing area and stacked on top of the relevant Ace in a stacking area, followed by the Three and the Four and so forth.

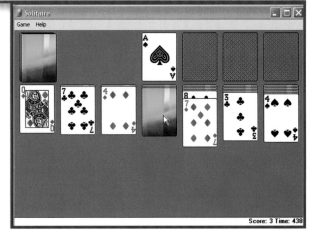

5

To deal some new cards three at a time, click the deck in the top-left corner. Drag-and-drop any suitable cards into the main playing area: in this case, the Ten of Hearts can go to the Jack of Clubs.

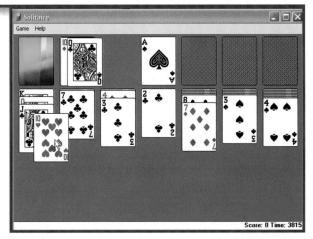

6

You can also drag a stack of cards from one column to another: in this case, the Eight of Clubs and the Seven of Diamonds from column five onto the Nine of Diamonds in column two. It's a little fiddly but the trick is to click onto the exposed upper-edge of the black Eight. The Seven remains locked to the Eight as you drag-and-drop the cards onto the red Nine.

When the deck has been fully dealt, a circle appears in the now-empty dealing area. Click the circle once to make the remaining deck jump back to the dealing area, and click again to start the dealing afresh. Keep moving cards to the Ace stacks whenever possible and see if you can clear the entire playing area.

Game

Deal

At any time, you can begin a fresh game by clicking the Game button on the Toolbar above the playing area. When the dropdown menu appears, click Deal.

Help

Contents

Solitaire

Play Solitaire

We're rather taking it for granted that you know how to play Solitaire! If not, consult the **Help menu**. This is excellent practice that will stand you in good stead when you come to work with more advanced application software later.
Select any topic in the left window pane and instructions appear to the right. When you've read as far as you can, click-and-hold the scrollbar on the right edge of the window and drag it slowly towards the bottom of the window. This has the effect of 'scrolling' the instructions so you can read them all. Alternatively, click the small arrow buttons at the top and bottom of the scrollbar [see p.60 for scrollbar details].
(You might also care to experiment with your mouse wheel at this point – roll it backwards and forwards to make the page scroll up and down.)

When you're finished, click the small, square cross button located at the very top-right corner of the Help

window. This closes the window and returns you to the game.
To close the Solitaire program itself, click the cross in the top-right corner of the window. There, it's as simple as that. Once you can comfortably drag-and-drop single or stacked cards from one column to another, deal from the deck and start a new game, you can truly say that you have mastered mouse control. What's more, you have learned a good deal about Windows (and windows) in the process without even trying!

Restraining the rodent

If, however, you really struggle with these practice exercises, there is a way to make the mouse more malleable. Proceed as follows:

1

Start

Control Panel

Printers and Other Hardware icon

Mouse icon

This takes you to a control area called Mouse Properties where you can train your mouse to behave more to your liking. In present circumstances, this means slowing it down. The appearance of this area depends upon the make and model of your mouse so you might not see exactly these screenshots. However, you should still be able to perform the following steps.

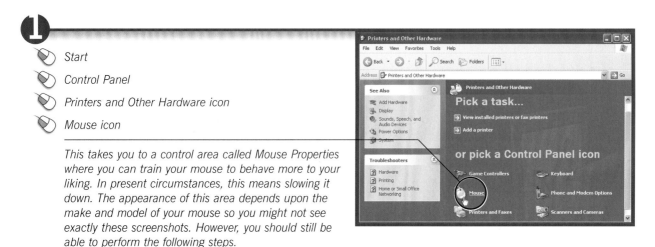

2

Pointer Options

Open the Pointer Options tab. A tab works like a divider in a folder, separating the contents into similar subject matter. To open a tab and view its contents, simply point at the title and click once.

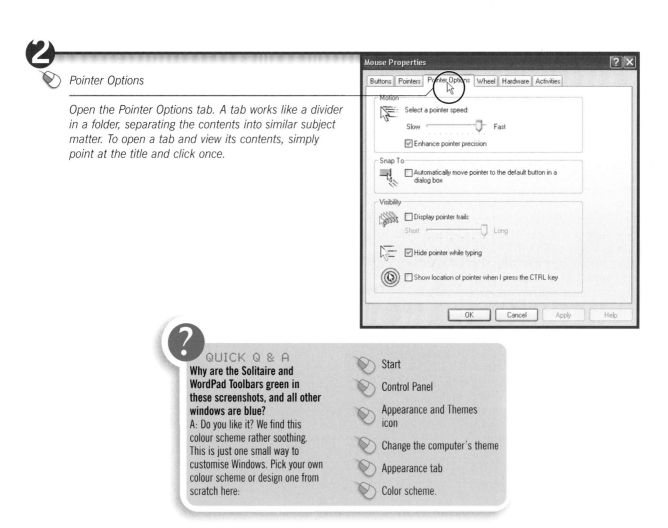

QUICK Q & A

Why are the Solitaire and WordPad Toolbars green in these screenshots, and all other windows are blue?

A: Do you like it? We find this colour scheme rather soothing. This is just one small way to customise Windows. Pick your own colour scheme or design one from scratch here:

Start

Control Panel

Appearance and Themes icon

Change the computer's theme

Appearance tab

Color scheme.

3

🖱 *[move slider]*

🖱 *Apply*

In the Motion area, you will see a graphical representation of a sliding scale. This relates to the sensitivity of the onscreen pointer in relation to your mouse (i.e. the closer the slider is to the Fast end of the spectrum, the faster the pointer travels across the screen). Click the slider control, drag it towards the left end of the scale, and release the mouse button just before it reaches Slow. Now slide the mouse around on its mat and note how you have to make big movements to move the pointer a small distance. If you like the effect, click the Apply button. If not, keep experimenting with the slider until you find a pointer speed that feels comfortable. Do not click the OK button until you have completed Step 4.

4

🖱 *Activities*

🖱 *[move slider]*

🖱 *Apply*

🖱 *OK*

Locating this next option can be tricky – it depends upon your make and model of mouse – but somewhere or other in one of the tabs there should lurk a way to slow the mouse's double-click speed. Increasing the delay is ideal if you have trouble double-clicking quickly enough. In this example, we found the option in the Activities tab. Drag the slider to the Slow end of the scale. You should now be able to test your new setting by double-clicking a folder (or a jack-in-the-box, or something similar). Experiment until you can open the folder or spring the jack with a double-click every time, even if it means using the very slowest setting. Finally, click the Apply button to confirm the change, and then click OK to close the Mouse Properties window.

PART Get to grips with your keyboard

Having looked in some detail at the mouse, we now turn to the keyboard. Although it's actually possible to operate a computer entirely with the keyboard – that is, the keyboard can do anything the mouse can do, and more besides – in practice you'll use the mouse and keyboard in tandem. Certainly, until speech recognition technology comes of age (current forecast: 12 June 2179), you'll use it every time you need to write a letter or type a command.

Anatomy of a keyboard

Like the mouse, a keyboard is an input device (i.e. it lets you interact with your computer). On pages 38-39, we see a standard-issue-type keyboard with 102 keys (plus three special Windows-specific keys).

To use it, you press the keys lightly, either one at a time or occasionally in combinations of two or three. If a combination is called for – let's say `Ctrl` + `S` – this means that you press *and hold* the `Ctrl` key and then press the `S` key with `Ctrl` still depressed.

A good combination to practise – if only because it's as hard as it gets – is `Ctrl` + `Alt` + `Del`. You can achieve this in several ways but you'll certainly need both hands. Our favoured approach is pressing and holding `Ctrl` with the ring finger on the left hand, then pressing and holding `Alt` with the index finger on the same hand, and finally pressing `Del` with any finger at all on the right hand. This three-key combination summons the useful Windows Task Manager (see page 88). For now, however, simply press the `Esc` key to make it go away.

You may or may not wish to learn to touch-type. If so, there are plenty of software programs around that can help; or, of course, you could seek out a tutor. With instruction, you will learn how to position your hands correctly and which finger to use for each key. But quite frankly we couldn't give a hoot about any of that right now. Feel free to use your keyboard in any manner you choose, even if it means stabbing each key with a solitary digit or poking them with a pencil.

Guide to the main sections of a computer keyboard.

Alphanumeric keys. These are the familiar typewriter keys laid out in the standard QWERTY arrangement (this refers to the first six keys on the top line). Here we find all the letters of the alphabet, numbers 0–9 and the essential punctuation symbols.

Within and around this block, there are several important keys that take some further explaining.

Function keys. *Labelled* [F1] *through to* [F12], *these keys conjure up certain functions in certain programs. We won't be bothering with them but there's one useful shortcut you should know: in Windows, the* [F1] *key acts as a shortcut to the Help & Support Centre.*

Spacebar. *This simply adds a space between words as you type.*

Esc. *The get-me-out-of-here-sharpish key. As a rule, the* [Esc] *key cancels the current operation or closes a dialogue box. Press one of the* [Windows] *keys to make the Start Menu pop up, and* [Esc] *to make it disappear again (yes, you've already done this back on page 29 but isn't it fun?).*

Tab. *Just like a typewriter, this indents paragraphs several spaces to the right.*

Caps Lock. *Press this key once and every letter key you type is printed in upper case; press it again to restore the keys to lower case. IF YOU LEAVE IT TURNED ON, YOUR TYPING WILL LOOK LIKE THIS.* [Caps lock] *is an example of a 'toggle' key – one press for on, another press for off.*

Shift. *You can also turn on upper case by pressing and holding this key as you type. Typically, you would capitalise the first letter of the first word in a sentence with the* [Shift] *key as it's quicker than turning the* [Caps lock] *function on and off again. The* [Shift] *key also lets you access the uppermost symbol on any key that has two possibilities. The number* [1] *key, for instance, prints an exclamation mark when you hold down* [Shift]. *Note that there are two* [Shift] *keys on your keyboard. They are entirely interchangeable.*

Ctrl. *Like the* [Shift] *key, this does nothing on its own but rather must be used in combination with other keys. For instance, pressing* [Ctrl] *and the letter* [S] *key together is a quick way of saving a document in most programs. There are two* [Ctrl] *keys.*

Windows. *Pressing the special* [Windows] *key, which is denoted by a flag, has the same effect as clicking the Start button. It also work as a combination key but we won't be calling upon its services. There are two* [Windows] *keys.*

Alt. *Yet another combination key that must be used in conjunction with other keys to have any effect. The second* [Alt] *key is actually called* [Alt Gr]. *We have absolutely no idea what it does and have never used it, so let's just give it a miss.*

Shift. *(see details bottom left)*

Backspace. *This key moves the cursor to the left one space at a time, and* **deletes** *any previous character. See the practical exercise with WordPad below for examples.*

Delete. *A key with many functions but in word processing it is generally used to erase the character immediately to the right of the current typing point. Again, we'll see how this works in a moment.*

Shortcut keys. *Many keyboards now feature an extra array of buttons that offer useful shortcuts e.g. launch an email program or web browser, navigate backwards and forwards through web pages, and adjust the speaker volume – all without touching the mouse. Nice to have but strictly non-essential.*

Lights. *Your keyboard also has three little status lights. One illuminates whenever the* Num lock *feature is active and another whenever* Caps lock *is on. The third relates to* Scroll lock*, a mysterious key that we have no knowledge of nor interest in.*

Numeric keypad. *With the keyboard's Num Lock function active (the* **default** *option when your computer starts; otherwise press* Num lock *) these calculator-style keys duplicate the number keys in the top row of the main section of the keyboard.*

With the Number Lock function disabled, the 2*,* 4*,* 6 *and* 8 *keys work just like a second set of arrow keys. The Home key takes you straight to the start of a line or the beginning of a web page; the End key takes you to the end. The Page Up/Page Down keys let you quickly scroll through an open document of web page on page, or screen, at a time.*

Shortcut. *This key has the same effect as clicking the right mouse button (see the explanation of right-clicking on [p30]).*

Enter. *This works primarily like the carriage return key on a traditional typewriter (i.e. starts a new line). There's a second* Enter *key tucked away at the very bottom-right corner of your keyboard. Also known as the Return key.*

Arrow keys. *This block of four arrows is primarily used to move the blinking cursor around the text on a printed page. What's a blinking cursor? Wait for [p.40].*

Practice makes perfect once again

OK, it's time to get a-clicking and put all this theory into practice. Again, we're going to jump the gun slightly and have you working with a Windows program, but just follow the directions closely and you'll have no difficulty. First, turn on your computer.

Start

All Programs

Accessories

WordPad

What we have here is the basic but functional word processor program that comes with Windows. You wouldn't write War and Peace *with WordPad but it can certainly help you master your keyboard with some simple exercises.*

First, click anywhere in the big white space. This, incidentally, is your computer's graphical representation of a sheet of paper. See that small vertical line blinking away in the top-left corner? This is technically known as the 'insertion point' because it's the point at which new text will be inserted, but we'll just call it the blinking cursor. Note that you still have a mouse pointer: just move the mouse around a bit and you'll see the familiar arrow dart around the screen. Confusing, isn't it? However, it's really important to recognise from the outset that these are quite distinct. The mouse pointer does what it always does – let's you control your computer – but the blinking cursor is contained within the page.

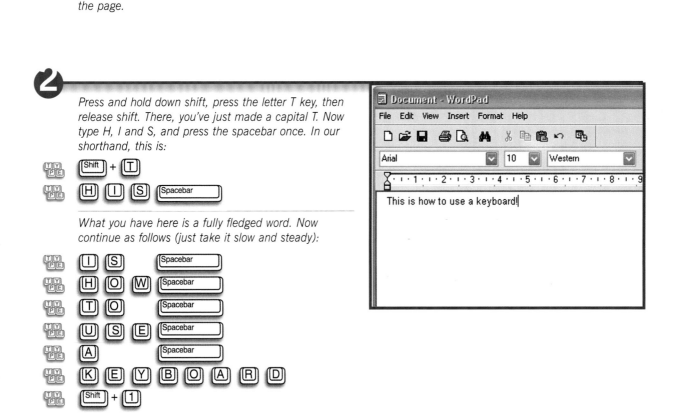

Press and hold down shift, press the letter T key, then release shift. There, you've just made a capital T. Now type H, I and S, and press the spacebar once. In our shorthand, this is:

Shift + T

H I S Spacebar

What you have here is a fully fledged word. Now continue as follows (just take it slow and steady):

I S Spacebar

H O W Spacebar

T O Spacebar

U S E Spacebar

A Spacebar

K E Y B O A R D

Shift + 1

3

If all went well, you should now be looking at this sentence in WordPad: 'This is how to use a keyboard!' Press [Enter] *once, and note how the blinking cursor moves down to a fresh line. Press* [Enter] *again and it moves down the page still further. Now press* [Backspace] *twice to return the blinking cursor to the end of your sentence.*

4

Experiment with the group of arrow keys. Each press of the [←] *key moves the blinking cursor one character to the left. Keep pressing it until you reach the beginning of the first word. Now use the* [→] *to move the blinking cursor back through the text. This time, however, pause when the blinking cursor is just to the right of the letter 'o' in the word 'to'. Press the* [Backspace] *key twice to delete the word.*
Now type [Shift] *+* [I].
Your sentences has changed to: 'This is how I use a keyboard!' That very simple edit shows the power of word processing.

5

This time, we want to change the word 'a' to 'my' but let's proceed slightly differently. Use the arrow keys to position the blinking cursor just to the left of the word 'a', then press [Del]. *The effect is the same – you're deleting a word – but this time you've rubbed out characters to the right of the blinking cursor rather than to the left. Now press* [M] *followed by* [Y].
Your sentence should now read: 'This is how I use my keyboard!' Keep practising with the arrow keys until you're comfortable positioning the blinking cursor anywhere within your sentence.

6

Move the blinking cursor to the right of the exclamation point and press [Enter] *twice. Now type:*

You should now have three rows of three numbers. Use the arrow keys to move the blinking cursor to the left of number 4.

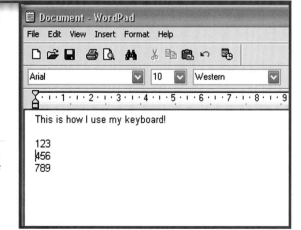

7

Now press the `Tab` key. This block of numbers will now be indented on the page. Move down to the beginning of the next block (i.e. to the left of number 7) and press `Tab` twice. This block will now be indented further. To remove the indents, position the blinking cursor just to the left of the numbers and use the `Backspace` key. Alternatively, position the blinking cursor at the very beginning of the line and use the `Del` key. This is simple formatting but already you can see how easy it is to arrange your words and numbers on a sheet of paper.

8

Finally, for now, return to your original sentence. Use the arrow keys to position the blinking cursor between the 'd' of 'keyboard' and the exclamation point. Now type:

Your new text is inserted straight into the original sentence, and everything to the right of the blinking cursor – in this case, just the explanation point – shuffles along to make space. You can't do that on a typewriter!
(Note that `@'` is one of those dual function keys where a simultaneous press of the `Shift` key would have printed the @ character instead of an apostrophe.)
Now go and make a cup of tea, but leave everything just as it is.

9

Ready for something a little fancier? You may have noticed that the mouse pointer changes shape depending on where in the window it happens to be. If you point at any of the buttons or menu options – File, Edit, View and so on – it looks like a normal pointer. However, if you move the pointer into the white page area, it changes to an 'I' shape. This is called an 'I-beam', and it offers an alternative way to manipulate text on the page.

Using the mouse, position the I-beam between the 'k' of 'break' and the exclamation point, and click once. The blinking cursor now moves to this position on the page. Don't worry if you miss a few times – just keep trying. If at any time the text becomes accidentally 'highlighted' (see Step 12 below), click on a blank spot on the page away from the text and the highlighting will disappear. Some people find the I-beam an easier way to position the blinking cursor within text than the arrow keys; others prefer the keyboard. Either way, you now have a choice.

Now move the mouse pointer to the beginning of your sentence and watch how it changes. As it approaches the first letter of the first word, it maintains an I-beam shape – but when you position it just to the left of the first word, it takes on the shape of an arrow. In contrast to the standard mouse pointer arrow, however, this arrow points to the right rather than to the left. What you have here is a 'selection tool'.

To see it in action, click once just as the mouse pointer turns from an I-beam into the selection tool. As if by magic, the entire line of text that it's pointing at becomes highlighted. This means that you can treat that text as a single unit and 'process' it in any way you choose. You might drag the sentence from one part of the page to another, for example, or change the font size or colour.

But for now, let's just delete our text. With the text highlighted, press the Del key. Now highlight any remaining text or numbers line-by-line with the selection tool and delete the lot until you have a blank page. Finally, close WordPad by clicking the cross in the top-right corner of the window. The program will ask you if you want to save changes to the document. Click the No button.

Sedating the keyboard

The thing that most people find trickiest about the keyboard is pressing and releasing the keys quickly enough. If you hold down a key for fractionally too long, the character is repeated on the pageeee (oops, there's an extra e or three right there). Having tried the exercises above, you'll know whether this applies to you. If so, here's how to make life a little easier. Proceed as follows:

Start

Control Panel

Printers and Other Hardware icon

Keyboard icon

This takes you to a control area called Keyboard Properties. The appearance of this area depends upon the make and model of your keyboard so you might not see exactly these screenshots. However, you should still be able to perform the following steps.

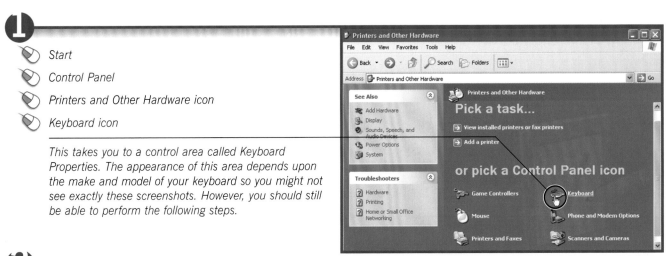

Speed

Open the Speed tab, or look in each tab until you find a section called Character Repeat. As a reminder, a tab is like a divider in a folder, separating the contents into related groups. To select a tab, simply point at the title – in this case Speed – and click once.

3

[test repeat rate]

Within the Character Repeat section, you will find a testing area that looks like a white rectangle. Point at this with mouse pointer and click once. A blinking cursor will appear within the box. This is your cue to start typing. Type any word or phrase and note how quickly a character repeats when you don't release the key quickly enough. If you run out of space, use the Backspace key to delete your text.

4

[move Repeat Delay slider]

[move Repeat Rate slider]

Apply

OK

If you find that your natural typing speed is too slow and extraneous letters keep appearing, you have two options. Repeat Delay governs how quickly a second character is printed after a key is pressed. The longer the delay, the less the chance of unwanted repeat characters. Repeat Rate determines how quickly subsequent characters then appear. The slower the rate, the fewer unwanted repeat characters. So, click-and-hold the slider controls in turn and move Repeat Delay to the Long end of the spectrum and Repeat Rate to Slow. Click anywhere in the test box again and you should find that your keyboard is now much more forgiving.
Click the Apply button to confirm the changes, and then click OK to close the Keyboard Properties window.

PART 2 Connecting the printer

It won't have escaped your notice that a couple of hunks of hardware are currently lying dormant on your desk or workstation. But now that you've had some practice with the mouse, keyboard and Windows itself, it's time to hook up the printer.

No two printers share exactly the same setup routine so you may have to interpret the following pictures and directions to suit. In particular, if you have opted for a laser printer rather than an inkjet, you will install a single toner cartridge instead of separate ink cartridges. As always, follow the manual's instructions closely. Or, if it's written in the worst kind of Techno-Pidgin, put it to one side and trust to common sense.

The ins and outs

For the first time, we're going to bring together hardware and the three types of software discussed on page 15.

Hardware. Pretty obvious, really – we need to connect the printer to the system unit. Printers generally use either a parallel cable or, much more commonly now, a USB cable. The latter is the case here. Note that printer manufacturers often fail to include a cable in the box – an unpardonable omission, in our opinion, that may see you scurrying down to your computer superstore before you can go any further.

Windows. Depending upon the make, model and age of your printer, Windows may or may not recognise the printer automatically. In other words, it may just work and it may just not. Why?

Driver. It all hinges on whether Windows has a built-in copy of the necessary driver software. Remember, a driver helps a computer make sense of its hardware components. If Windows is lacking, no matter – you will find the driver you need on a CD-ROM supplied with the printer.

Program. Click the Print button in any program and whatever you see on screen – a letter, say, or a full-colour digital image – materialises on paper. It's as simple as that. A printer without any programs to keep it busy is a dull thing indeed. Moreover, many printers ship with extra programs that let you design greetings card and t-shirt transfers and so forth.

Unpacking and setting up

With lots of moving parts, printers are vulnerable to damage during transit. This is why they usually arrive trussed up like oven-ready turkeys. Your first task is to extract the device from its polystyrene shell, dig out the manual, and unpeel all the sticky tape. Next, attach any supplied paper input and output trays or feeders. Now pause and follow the instructions very carefully indeed. You might be told to plug the printer straight into the system unit, switch it on and see what happens; or you might have a couple of other preparatory steps to complete first.

In this example, the printer comes with a separate print head – a device that controls the flow of ink from the cartridges onto the page – that must be installed prior to use. However, some printer manufacturers use a different system whereby each ink cartridge incorporates its own print head. In this case, Step 2 will not apply.

With the computer turned off, connect the stubby square end of a USB cable to the port on the rear of the printer and the flat rectangular end to a USB port on the system unit. Connect the power cable to the mains electricity and turn the printer on.

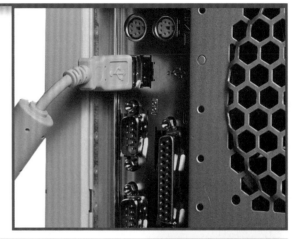

After a few moments, the internal print head holder inside the printer moves to a central position. Open the front cover and raise the locking lever. Now carefully remove the print head from its packaging and, taking great care not to touch the nozzles or electrical contacts, slide the device into position.

Now lock the print head into position with the lever and install the ink cartridges. This printer has four: black, cyan, magenta and yellow. Again, follow the directions carefully and handle the ink with care. Close the cover when the cartridges are all in place. Finally, turn the printer off in preparation for the next procedure.

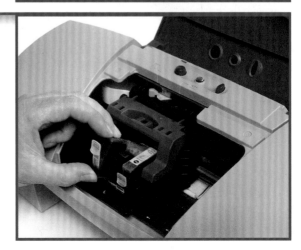

Installing the driver

The printer is now physically ready to go, but it still needs a driver, and this is where we step slightly into the unknown. Windows XP is particularly adept at recognising new hardware without a fuss, and often you can get going simply by plugging a device in and turning it on. If Windows has the drivers it needs, installation is automatic; if not, it prompts for the CD-ROM.

However, in our example, the manual advises that you should install the driver software *before* turning on the printer. That's the procedure we will follow here.

With the computer and printer both turned off but connected via a USB cable as described above, turn on the computer and wait for Windows to start up. Do not turn on the printer. When you see the Windows Desktop, place the CD-ROM that contains the driver software in the CD drive, printed or label-side up. Do be sure to use the correct CD-ROM if two or more are supplied – it should say 'setup software' or something similar. The CD-ROM should now start running automatically.

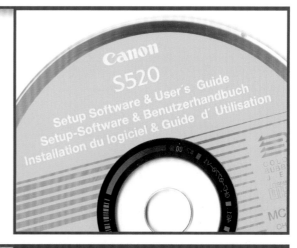

The first thing we see here is a licence agreement. Read this and click Yes (or Accept or whatever the 'I agree, let's get on with it' option happens to be). If you click No, the installation program will close.

*This is what we like to see – a big red button called Install! Click this now and wait for Windows to **copy** the required files from the CD-ROM to the computer's hard disk.*

We are now prompted to turn the printer on. Remember, the printer and system unit are already connected with a USB cable. After a little more file copying, we are rewarded with a success message. Click OK and the printer is just about ready to roll. This would be a good time to put some blank A4 paper in the input tray.

Final tweaks

Modern inkjet printers are capable of producing fantastically high quality images, including 'photo-realistic' prints that are all-but indistinguishable from professionally developed snapshots.

However, you will almost certainly have to perform a little routine maintenance on your printer right now to ensure that it's properly set up to produce pin-sharp prints. In this case, the manual suggests, nay, insists upon, 'aligning the print heads'. Again, your printer may use a rather different procedure but the aim and results will be similar.

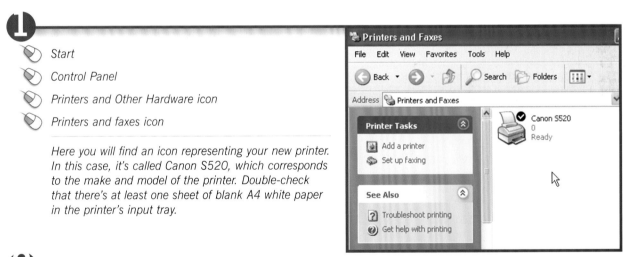

Start

Control Panel

Printers and Other Hardware icon

Printers and faxes icon

Here you will find an icon representing your new printer. In this case, it's called Canon S520, which corresponds to the make and model of the printer. Double-check that there's at least one sheet of blank A4 white paper in the printer's input tray.

Canon S520 icon

Printing Preferences

Right-clicking the printer icon gives you access to some menu options. Printing Preferences is where we want to be right now.

Maintenance

Print Head Alignment

In the Maintenance tab, we find an option to align the print heads (you may have to root around a bit to find this). Click the button and settle back while the printer generates a test sheet.

A dialogue box asks if the page has printed. Assuming that it has, click Yes. You are now prompted to examine a few printed columns and specify which blocks of colour are uniform in appearance. Don those reading spectacles and take your time here, as the accuracy of your future printing depends on these responses. To make your selections, click each column in turn in the dialogue box – the layout corresponds to the printed page – and use the up and down arrows to select the correct boxes. Fiddly? You bet. Then click OK. That's it, you're done. Thankfully, many inkjet printers now perform these maintenance tasks automatically.

Testing your printer

Your printer will have come with one or two programs that help you enhance digital pictures, produce greetings cards and the like. You can install and experiment with these programs now if you like or wait for the application software sections later. In the meantime, having performed any maintenance tasks specified in the manual, let's test that your printer is working properly.

Start

All Programs

Accessories

WordPad

Yes, it's back to trusty old WordPad again. Just type anything you fancy and click the Print button on the Toolbar. Out of your printer will pop a page that matches the screen. This is what's meant by the acronym WYSIWYG, pronounced wizziwig: What You See Is What You Get.

Start

 All Programs

Accessories

Paint

Let's add a little colour now. Paint is a rudimentary drawing program included with Windows but it fits our current needs quite nicely. Click on the paintbrush icon on the left side of the screen, then click any of the coloured boxes at the foot of the screen to 'pick up' a colour, and move the mouse around to paint in the white area of the screen. Add some new colours and play around with the other drawing tools. When you have produced perfection, or a perfect mess, click File on the Toolbar, followed by Print and then Print again in the pop-up dialogue box (depending on your printer this may look different on your computer from our screenshot).
And there you have it: digital artwork made simple.

Parallel lines

If your printer doesn't have a USB port and/or you would rather use the parallel interface, the 'plug-and-play' routine described above may not work. In such cases, use the following method:

 Start

 Control Panel

 Printers and Other Hardware icon

Add a printer

*This launches the Add Printer Wizard. Follow the step-by-step directions, being sure to specify that you're installing a local rather than a network printer (which would be connected to another computer). Also remove the tick next to 'Automatically detect and install my **Plug and Play** printer' box by clicking the box. This, incidentally, is an example of **'checking'** an option: one click adds a tick, or check mark; another click removes it.*

However, we must stress that it is far preferable to use a USB-capable printer and cable. Installation is easier and the printer itself will do its stuff faster.

PART 2 Connecting the scanner

Printers may be devilishly complex devices but scanners are comparatively simple. Essentially, a flatbed scanner – which looks like a small photocopier – takes a digital picture of whatever you place under the lid. This picture is then transferred to your computer, whereupon you can view and tweak it with an image-editing program. It needs no routine maintenance beyond an occasional wipe with a cloth, no refills, and should serve you well for years.

There are other types of scanners, notably handheld devices that you pass over a page, but flatbeds are the norm for home use.

Installation

Thanks to a universal driver standard called *TWAIN*, it is possible to 'import' an image from a scanner into all manner of programs. You might wish to scan a snapshot and enhance it on your computer by digitally removing flash-induced red-eye, for

A scanner takes digital pictures that can be imported into programs and saved as files on your computer's hard disk.

Don't forget to 'unlock' your scanner before attempting to use it!

example; or convert a newspaper article into editable text (a process known as Optical Character Recognition). Even word processors and spreadsheet programs can usually import images straight from a scanner.

Virtually all modern scanners now use the USB interface, which makes installation a breeze. However, the device will likely be protected by all manner of packaging and tape upon arrival. All this is easily removed, but there's one very important task that you _must_ perform. The scanning mechanism itself, which is located under the glass plate, is secured during transit. You must locate and unlock the release mechanism before you use your scanner. As always, check the manual for directions. Some releases, as in our example, are commendably obvious, but your device may have a tiny catch tucked away on the underside of the scanner's housing.

Installing the driver, which is of course essential to get your scanner working, is very straightforward. With your computer turned on and windows running, first connect the scanner to the system unit with a USB cable, and then turn it on. Windows will launch something called the Found New Hardware Wizard, which is essentially just a step-by-step installation routine. Ensure that the default 'Install the software automatically' option is checked – if not, click the little circle to check it – and pop the driver CD-ROM in its drive. Now click the Next button and follow the directions.

Let a Windows Wizard do the work.

PART 3 Windows XP

As we remarked earlier, Windows is a graphical, point-and-clicky, touchy-feely kind of operating system. The upshot is that once you've mastered a few simple concepts, your computer becomes remarkably easy to use (this wasn't always the case but the XP generation has helped matters enormously). Almost regardless of what you want to do, the same rules and steps apply.

Now, you could write an entire manual on the Windows operating system and how to use it – and many people have – but our aim here, in the time-honoured principle of learning to walk before you can run, is to take you through the basics. By the end of the chapter, you will, we trust, feel comfortable working within the Windows environment.

PART 3 Key concepts

Windows typically provides ten ways to do anything and is loaded with smart shortcuts and time-saving tricks. But that way lies complexity and confusion. Here we stick to the most logical and straightforward, if not necessarily the quickest, methods of getting from A to E

The Desktop

When you turn on your computer and Windows starts, your starting point is always the Desktop. The key areas are these:

Icons

Clickable links to programs and folders. In this example, there are five on view, but your computer's Desktop may look rather different depending on how your supplier has customised your system. Note that if you point at an icon without clicking, you'll get a pop-up bubble with a little information about it. This is called a screen tip.

My Documents *A folder on the hard disk used to store files that you create when you work with programs. You can also access all other folders from here. We'll work with My Documents in detail on page 63.*

My Computer *A quick way to find information about your computer's hardware, including its drives.*

My Network Places *Only relevant if your computer is linked to other computers or connected to the internet (as it will be in Part 4).*

Internet Explorer *A web browser. That is to say, the program that you'll use to view web pages on the internet.*

Recycle Bin *An important one. When you delete a file from your computer's hard disk, instead of disappearing irretrievably it actually gets stored in the Recycle Bin. This effectively gives you a chance to recover any file deleted by mistake – and believe us, you'll delete plenty of files by mistake as you work with your computer!*

Background *Just a picture to brighten up your day. In fact, it can be any picture you like.*

The Start Menu *See over the page for a detailed description of this important item.*

QUICK Q & A

Q: The only icon I have on my Desktop is the Recycle Bin.

A: No problem. Look for My Documents, My Computer, My Network Places and Internet Explorer in the Start menu. right-click each one in turn and check the Show on Desktop option.

Taskbar A strip running across the bottom of the screen that shows you what's going on. At the far left, we find the Start button, which we'll consider in detail in a moment. At the far right is the Notification Area. Right now, there is probably only a clock on show but many programs install an icon here to reassure you that they're beavering away in the *background*. Most antivirus programs, for example, lodge an icon here. Windows itself also uses the Notification Area to keep you informed about updates and offer occasional snippets of information.

The central part of the Taskbar is used to display buttons that relate to current activity. Let's see it in action now.

My Computer icon

This opens a window with information about your computer. Ignore its contents for now and note instead that an important change has occurred on the Taskbar. A button called (no surprises here) My Computer has appeared.
OK, it doesn't look much like a button but try clicking it once. The My Computer window disappears from your screen and you're back to the plain Desktop again. All that's happened here is that My Computer has been 'minimised' to the Taskbar (i.e. the window is still open but temporarily reduced to a button). Click the button again and up pops the My Computer window.

Minimise My Computer once more with a click on the Task bar button and open the Recycle Bin by double-clicking its Desktop icon:

Recycle Bin icon

Now there are two buttons on the Taskbar.

Practice clicking these buttons to manipulate the windows. For instance, you can keep both windows minimised at the same time, or have one open on the Desktop with the other minimised, or have both windows open on the Desktop simultaneously. In this case, one window – the 'active' window – will partially obscure the other but you can easily reverse the order by clicking the button that corresponds to the half-hidden window. Note that the button corresponding to the topmost window looks as if it has been depressed.

As we shall soon see, the ability to work with multiple folders/programs/tasks at the same time is central to the Windows operating system. The Taskbar is the tool you need to monitor and control your windows as you work.

My Network Places

Owner

The Start Menu

You could sit and stare at the Desktop all day, but to do something useful you need the Start button and its corresponding menu. Click it once and you'll see something like this. What can it all mean?

Current User *Here you see your name and a picture of your choosing. Or, rather, you don't but will on page 131.*

 Internet
Internet Explorer

Pinned Programs *This section contains fixed links to certain programs. Internet Explorer (a web browser) and Outlook Express (an e-mail program) are always 'pinned' here but you can add other programs, too.*

 E-mail
Outlook Express

Frequently Used Programs *This section updates all the time to reflect the six programs you use most, aside from any that appear in the pinned programs section.*

 Paint Shop Pro 6

 Tour Windows XP

 Windows Media Player

 Windows Movie Maker

 WordPad

 Windows Messenger

All Programs *Click here to access a full list of all the software installed on your computer. We were here earlier in the mouse and keyboard sections when we launched Solitaire and WordPad. A right-pointing arrow next to a menu entry indicates that the entry can be expanded. Some of these 'sub-menus' can themselves be further expanded (see above). Note that to save time you merely have to point at an entry on the Start Menu to make it expand; only click an entry when you want to launch the program.*

As you install more and more software on your computer, you'll begin to see the attraction of the Pinned Programs and Frequently Used Programs sections of the Start Menu. They provide useful shortcuts to the programs that you use most often and save you always having to root through the All Programs list.

 All Programs

start

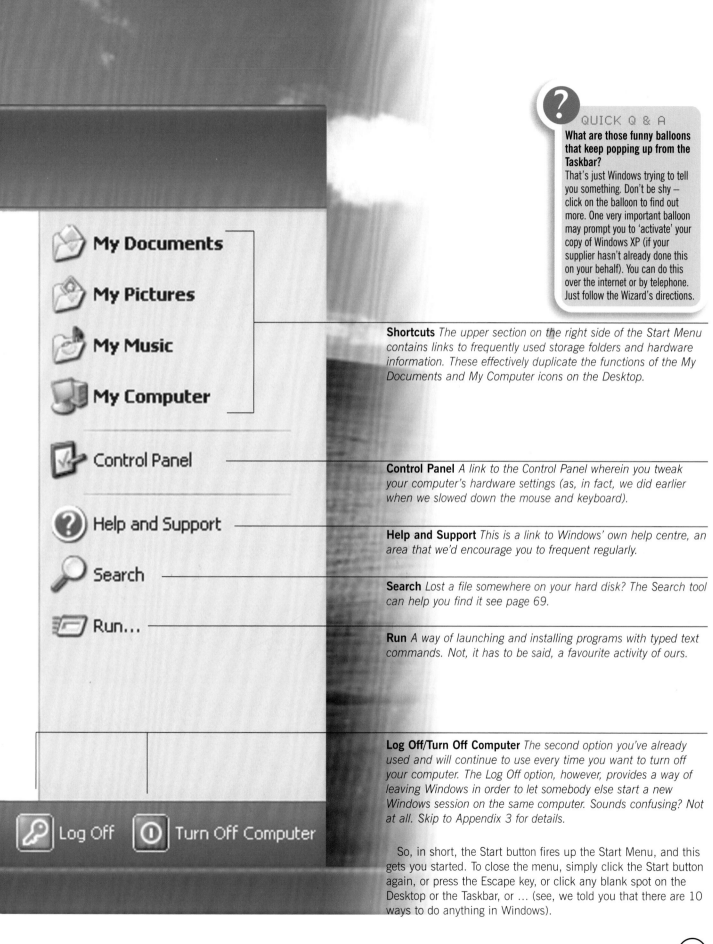

QUICK Q & A

What are those funny balloons that keep popping up from the Taskbar?
That's just Windows trying to tell you something. Don't be shy — click on the balloon to find out more. One very important balloon may prompt you to 'activate' your copy of Windows XP (if your supplier hasn't already done this on your behalf). You can do this over the internet or by telephone. Just follow the Wizard's directions.

My Documents

My Pictures

My Music

My Computer

Control Panel

Help and Support

Search

Run...

Log Off　**Turn Off Computer**

Shortcuts *The upper section on the right side of the Start Menu contains links to frequently used storage folders and hardware information. These effectively duplicate the functions of the My Documents and My Computer icons on the Desktop.*

Control Panel *A link to the Control Panel wherein you tweak your computer's hardware settings (as, in fact, we did earlier when we slowed down the mouse and keyboard).*

Help and Support *This is a link to Windows' own help centre, an area that we'd encourage you to frequent regularly.*

Search *Lost a file somewhere on your hard disk? The Search tool can help you find it see page 69.*

Run *A way of launching and installing programs with typed text commands. Not, it has to be said, a favourite activity of ours.*

Log Off/Turn Off Computer *The second option you've already used and will continue to use every time you want to turn off your computer. The Log Off option, however, provides a way of leaving Windows in order to let somebody else start a new Windows session on the same computer. Sounds confusing? Not at all. Skip to Appendix 3 for details.*

So, in short, the Start button fires up the Start Menu, and this gets you started. To close the menu, simply click the Start button again, or press the Escape key, or click any blank spot on the Desktop or the Taskbar, or … (see, we told you that there are 10 ways to do anything in Windows).

Getting comfortable with windows

Whenever you open a program or perform a task on your computer, the action takes place inside a self-contained box on your monitor screen, called a window. Each open window is (more or less) independent of all others and, as we have seen, you can switch between windows using the Taskbar. Here we look at a typical window's key features.

 My Computer

QUICK Q & A

Q: How do I see more/less on my monitor screen?
A: This is down to screen resolution. The lower the resolution, the bigger everything appears but the less room you have for lots of windows; increase the resolution and windows and icons shrink, but you can squeeze more onto the screen at any one time. Consult your monitor's manual to check which resolutions it 'supports' (i.e. can work with), and experiment here:

- Start
- Control Panel
- Appearance and Themes icon
- Change the screen resolution
- [move screen resolution slider]
- Apply

Title Bar. *The shaded top edge of a window displays the name of the program or process in question. The Title Bar also has three important little buttons.*

▬ *The first button minimises the window (i.e. turns it into a button on the Taskbar). To restore it, you click the Taskbar button.*

▢ *The middle button maximises the window so that it takes up all available screen space. Click it again to restore the window to its original size.*

☒ *The final button should be familiar by now: it closes the window.*

You can also click any point on the title bar, hold down the mouse button, drag the window to a different position on the screen and then drop it in place (as we saw back on page 31). Don't forget that you can resize windows, too (see page 30).

Menu bar *A number of clickable menus containing organised control and configuration options. The contents of each menu depends upon the program or process. WordPad, for instance, has a rather different set of menus.*

Toolbar *Clickable buttons. Again, these relate to the program or the process and vary considerably.*

Scrollbar *When it's not possible to see the entire contents of a window all at one time, a scrollbar appears. This lets you scroll up and down and through the window. Either click-and-drag the scrollbar slider or click the little arrows above and below the scrollbar (or to the left and right in the case of a horizontal scrollbar).*

Pane *Windows may be sub-divided into separate sections. Each section is, predictably enough, called a window pane.*

In Windows, you can only do something (perform a task, click an icon, type some text, whatever) within one window, the 'active' window, at any one time. You can tell which window is currently active in two ways: a depressed Taskbar button, and an emboldened title bar. In the screen shot on page 57, for instance, the My Computer window is clearly active. To make the Recycle Bin active, you would click its Taskbar button.

When you have two or more windows open, you can use the Taskbar to automatically arrange them on screen – a useful alternative to manually resizing your windows. Right-click any blank spot on the Taskbar (i.e. avoid any buttons) and select one of these options: Cascade Windows, Tile Windows Horizontally or Tile Windows Vertically. You can even close any open window by right-clicking its Taskbar button and selecting Close.

Tiling your windows is one way of keeping several open on screen at the same time. Remember, though, that you can only work with the active window at any given time.

PART 3 Files and folders

Sooner or later, you're going to create something on your computer that you want to save. You have a choice of storage locations, as we'll see in the very next section, but first it helps to get a handle on the notion of files and folders – and, specifically, how Windows XP works with them.

Here we see a hierarchy of folders in the left window pane with files within a selected folder displayed in the right pane. Your computer has many, many levels of files within folders within folders within folders . . .

So what's a file?

A file is any single self-contained chunk of information stored in a digital format. A letter written on a word processor and saved to the hard disk is a file; an image created on or copied from a scanner or a digital camera is a file; a computer-generated sound recording is a file; a digital video clip is a file; even a computer program is a file (or, rather, a collection of files).

Although all files are essentially just a collection of 1s and 0s – that is, *binary data* – your computer has to be able to tell one file from another. Thus every file has two parts: a file name, and a file extension that tells the computer something about its format. When you make your own files, you choose the name as you go along, and you can be as creative or pedantic as you like. The extension, however, ties the file to a particular program or type of program, and needs to be chosen with care (when indeed there is a choice at all). An extension is usually 2, 3 or 4 letters long and tacked on to the file name proper with a dot separating them.

For example, let's say you write a letter in Word, the popular word processing program, and call it 'Hi Mum'. Word's default file extension is '.doc', so this file's full title becomes 'Hi Mum.doc'. Now, any other computer with a recent version of Word installed can open, read and edit this file. You will, of course, be able to open it yourself whenever you like.

Some file formats and their associated extensions are proprietary. The '.doc' format belongs to Microsoft, for instance, which effectively means that only Word and other Microsoft programs can create or open '.doc' files. (Actually, some other word processors can work with '.doc' files but only by means of special import filters.)

However, many file formats are non-proprietary, which means that they are compatible with a wider range of programs. A sound recording, for instance, might be saved in the common .wav format and opened with just about any program capable of playing sound files. A web page – which is, after all, just another file – will generally have an .htm or .html extension, and any web browser the world over can view it.

The only time you really have to worry about file formats and extensions is when you want to share your files. That is, if you write a report in Word and save it with the '.doc' file extension, you should first ensure that all intended recipients of the file have a copy of Word on their computers. Failing that, you can choose an alternative non-proprietary file extension. In the case of text files, this would generally be '.txt' or '.rtf'.

OK, so what's a folder?

A folder is a file holder. Just as you might keep your paper documents in a series of folders in a filing cabinet, so on a computer you save files in the virtual equivalent of folders. A folder is just an organisational tool – a gimmick, if you like – designed to make file management intuitive and sensible.

Moreover, Windows lets you work with a hierarchy of 'nested' files and folders (i.e. files within folders within folders within folders, and so on, more or less forever). The advantage is that you can organise your work in such a way that it's easy to retrieve any individual file in moments. When you consider that your computer's hard disk can easily hold *millions* of files, good file management is truly essential.

Say you write a letter to your bank manager on your computer, print out a hard copy and post it. You're going to want to keep a copy on your computer, and that means saving the letter as a file. But where, exactly? Let's imagine that you already have a folder called Home Finances. This sounds like a good starting point. However, you also keep details of household bills and standing orders and hire purchase agreements in here. What you need is a sub-folder within Home Finances called something like Bank Correspondence. Now *that* would be a good place to store your letter. Even if you completely forget where you've saved it, you should be able to track it down months or even years down the line.

But where do all these folders come from? The answer is that you make them yourself as you go along. It's time for some practical exercises.

Making folders

Here we will create a brand new folder on your computer's hard disk.

My Documents icon

Windows provides a very useful 'top-level' folder called My Documents. You'll find its icon on the Desktop. Double-click this icon to open the folder and inside you'll find two or three sub-folders: My Music, My Pictures and, perhaps, My Videos. These are simply the recommended locations for saving music, image and video files respectively. What you will not find is a Home Finances folder. So let's make one.

Make a new folder

This option is found in the left window pane in an area called File and Folder Tasks. If by chance your My Documents folder looks rather different from our screenshot and the File and Folder Tasks area is not visible, click the Folders button on the Toolbar (we'll be covering the different ways to view and work with folders later).

Home Finances

*A new folder appears in the right-hand side of the My Documents window. It's given title is, boringly, New Folder, but we can change that. Because the words 'New Folder' are automatically highlighted at the point of creating the folder, all you have to do is **overtype** a new title. In this case, we're calling it Home Finances.*

New Folder icon

Rename this folder

 Home Finances

This step only applies if Step 3 goes wrong and you didn't manage to rename the folder while 'New Folder' was highlighted. Select New Folder by clicking its icon once. Now look in the left window pane and you'll see an option to Rename this folder. Click this and once again the folder's title becomes highlighted. Now just type in the new name and press the Enter key. Any folder can be renamed in this manner.

Home Finances icon

Make a new folder

 Bank Correspondence

Following the example discussed above, we now want to create a sub-folder within Home Finances called Bank Correspondence. Double-click the Home Finances folder icon to open the folder (which is, of course, currently empty). Now create and name a new folder just as in Steps 2 and 3 above. Once again, you can easily rename the folder as in Step 4 if anything goes wrong.

Saving and opening files

You now have a suitable home for a letter to your bank manager. Its file path (a rather ungainly method of specifying the location of any file or folder) is this:

My Documents\Home Finances\Bank Correspondence

Each slash (\) indicates that the following folder is a sub-folder of the previous folder. What you do not yet have is the letter itself, so let's create and save just such a file now.

 Start

 All Programs

 Accessories

 WordPad

Yes, it's back to trusty WordPad again. There's every chance that your computer system came with a fully-fledged word processor like Microsoft Word but this will do for now. Open the program and type a letter to your bank manager. Or rather, to save time, type anything you like, even just a word or two.

 File

 Save As

In some ways, this is the most important lesson in the entire manual. What you're about to do is save a file. Once saved, this file – any file – will be stored safely on your computer's hard disk. But until it is saved, the file doesn't really exist. A sudden power cut would obliterate it.
You'll find the File menu button on the far left of the Menu Bar. Click it once and down drops a drop-down menu. Move the mouse pointer down through the menu until Save As is highlighted, and then click once.

 Home Finances icon

 Open

The Save As window is where you pick a location for your file. As it happens, Windows expects you to save files in the My Documents folder or a folder within it, hence My Documents appears in the Save in: box automatically. Below this, you can see all the folders located within My Documents – and right there is your Home Finances folder. Click its icon to select it and then click the Open button.

Bank Correspondence icon

 Open

Now the Home Finances folder appears in the Save in: box and below it you can see the Bank Correspondence sub-folder. Select this now and click Open.

 File name box

 Letter to bank manager requesting a loan

You have navigated successfully to the Bank Correspondence folder, which is where your file will now be saved. In the File name: box near the bottom of the window, the word 'Document' appears. This is WordPad's default suggestion for file names but it would be a spectacularly uninspiring choice here. So, click once in the File name box to select 'Document' and replace it with your own file name. Click the Save button when you're through.

 [edit file]

 ⊠

The Save As window disappears and you're back with your document again. Check the window's Title Bar and you'll see that it displays your chosen file name – proof that your file saving has been successful. You could print the file at this point (click the Print icon on the Toolbar), or close it (click the cross in the top-right corner of the window). However, try this first. Make some small change to the letter, such as adding or deleting a word or two. We replaced 'Thanks awfully' with 'Thanks very much'. Now try to close the window.

 No

WordPad identifies that the file you are currently trying to close is not the same in every respect as the file you originally saved with this file. This means that the original file is about to be overwritten by (that is, deleted and replaced with) this amended version, and so the program asks you whether this is indeed what you intend. It's a crucial point: if you click No, the changes you just made will be lost and the file will revert to its original form; click Yes and the file will be saved exactly as is and the original file will be lost forever. In this case, click No. See page 89 for more on saving and overwriting files.

Start

 All Programs

 Accessories

 WordPad

 File

 Open

Let's now suppose that you wish to find and read this file at some later date. We'll show you two ways to go about this. First, launch WordPad and click Open from the File menu.

 Home Finances icon

 Open

 Bank Correspondence icon

 Open

 Letter to bank manager requesting a loan icon

Open

Now it's a case of navigating through folders until you find the letter. When you see your target file, select it and click Open once more.

 My Documents icon

 Home Finances icon

 Bank Correspondence icon

Alternatively, you can locate and open this (or any) file through the My Documents folder. Double-click the My Documents icon on the Desktop to open the folder in a window, and then double-click the Home Finances icon within it. Repeat with Bank Correspondence. Again, this is simply navigating through folders.

Letter to bank manager requesting a loan icon

Finally, double-click the icon that represents your file. This launches the WordPad program and opens your file simultaneously.

One point to note: Windows associates file formats with particular programs, and it's always the default program that launches when you double-click a file. In this case, WordPad happens to be the default program for .rtf files – but if there was a second program capable of handling text files installed on this computer, like Word, it's possible that it would be associated with .rtf files instead. In other words, opening a file does not necessarily launch the program it was created in.

Deleting, recovering and searching for files. Oh, and a shortcut too

Windows offers two ways to manipulate files and folders: Task view and Folders view. The former, a new approach only introduced with Windows XP, is designed to make it easier and faster to perform common tasks. But is it? Let's find out.

 My Documents icon

Home Finances icon

The left pane of this window has links to things that Windows thinks you might want to do. These include renaming or moving a folder or file, copying it, sharing it with other people who use this computer, or e-mailing a folder's contents to a contact. You can also delete files and folders here. We'll do that now.

 Delete this folder

Yes

With Home Finances folder selected in the window, click Delete this folder in the left pane. Up pops a box asking for final confirmation. Click Yes. And that's it – your Home Finances folder and all its contents has gone for good.

 Recycle Bin icon

Home Finances icon

Restore this item

Actually, not quite. Remember what we said about the Recycle Bin earlier (p.56)? Double-click its Desktop icon now and inside you will find the deleted folder. Select this folder with a click and then click Restore this item in the left pane. As if by magic, the folder now reappears in your My Documents folder. It has been un-deleted.

Folders

Back at the My Documents window, click the Folders button on the Toolbar. The left pane changes to show the hierarchical structure of your computer's folders. This is more how Windows used to look. To expand any folder, click the '+' sign to the left of its icon. Although this is ideal for in-depth navigation, the chances are that pretty soon you'll lose track of where you are. This is why we heartily recommend sticking to the Task view! Still, try to locate your letter file while you're here. Then click the Folders button once again to return to Task view.

Start

Search

Documents

Let's suppose that you haven't been terribly rigorous with your file management and have somehow misplaced your letter. Windows has a built-in search facility which you can access from the Start Menu. To speed things up, it helps if you specify what type of file you are looking for. In this case, it's a document. However, if you're not sure, just click the 'All files and folders' option. Ignore the daft dog.

[keywords]

Search

You are now invited to enter any information that might narrow the search further. We'll use two keywords: letter and bank. You can also tell the dog, sorry, Windows when you last modified (worked with) the file. Click the Search button.

Letter to bank manager requesting a loan icon

Hey presto, there it is. Double-click the icon to open the file in Word Pad and immediately save it afresh in a sensible location that you won't forget (i.e. in a folder called Bank Correspondence within a folder called Home Finances within the My Documents folder).

Letter to bank manager requesting a loan icon

Finally, one time-saving tip we just can't resist. When you work with particular folders or files frequently, you can place a shortcut to them right on the Desktop. This saves you having to navigate through the My Documents folder every time. Open the My Documents folder as before, find your letter, right-click the icon and hold down the mouse button. Now, still holding that right mouse button down, drag the icon out of the My Documents window and onto a clear space on the Desktop.

Create Shortcuts Here

Release the right mouse button and up pops a menu. Point at Create Shortcuts Here to select it and click once (back to the left mouse button now). The original file stays put in the Bank Correspondence folder but now there's a new icon on the Desktop. This, we stress, is not the file itself but merely a shortcut, or link, to the original file. You can now open the file at any time by double-clicking its shortcut.

Desktop

Arrange Icons By

Auto Arrange

Right-*click any clear spot on the Desktop and ensure that the Auto Arrange option has a tick next to it (if not, click it). This forces your icons to arrange themselves in nice, neat columns on the Desktop. If Auto Arrange is unchecked, incidentally, you can arrange your Desktop icons yourself. Just drag-and-drop them wherever you like.*

Different views

Using My Documents, you can also view your files and folders in several different ways: just select from the options in the View menu on the Menu Bar. Feel free to experiment. Filmstrip view is perfect for previewing pictures (available only in the special My Pictures folder).

2

Thumbnails gives you a small representation of the file.

3

Icons is ideal for dragging-and-dropping files.

4

Tile view basically means bigger icons.

5

Use List or Details view when you need fuller information about your files.

Copying files and folders

You will sometimes want to move a file or a whole folder from one location on the hard disk to another. This is very easily accomplished in Windows in a number of ways. We'll break our keep-it-simple rule temporarily to look at three different methods, but only to give you the chance to find the best one for you.

 1

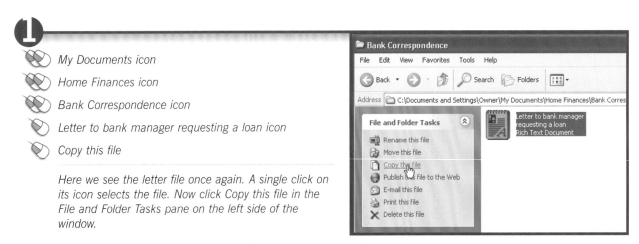

- *My Documents icon*
- *Home Finances icon*
- *Bank Correspondence icon*
- *Letter to bank manager requesting a loan icon*
- *Copy this file*

Here we see the letter file once again. A single click on its icon selects the file. Now click Copy this file in the File and Folder Tasks pane on the left side of the window.

 2

- *(+) My Documents*
- *My Music icon*
- *Copy*

When the Copy Items window appears, click the tiny '+' sign next to My Documents to expand the folder (i.e. show all its sub-folders). Then click on the My Music folder, and click the Copy button. This immediately saves a copy of your letter in the My Music folder while leaving the original file safely stored in the Bank Correspondence folder.

 3

- *My Documents icon*
- *My Music icon*

But just to be sure, have a look in the My Music folder. There it is. Let's leave it there for time being and look at an alternative file management method.

One of the reasons why we encouraged you to play Solitaire early on was to practise your drag-and-drop skills. Remember how you dragged playing cards from one column and dropped them on another? Well, you can also drag-and-drop files and folders, both within a single window or between windows. We'll look at these in turn.

Folders

(+) Home Finances

Starting precisely where you left off in the previous exercise – that is, with the My Music folder open – click the Folders button on the Toolbar. This replaces the Tasks pane on the left side of the window with a hierarchical Folders view of your computer. Now very carefully click the little + sign next to Home Finances. (If you accidentally click the Home Finances icon instead, just click the Back button on the Toolbar and try again.) The Bank Correspondence folder should now be visible in the Folders section of the left window pane.

Sample Music icon

Now right-*click the Sample Music icon and* hold down the mouse button. *Drag the Sample Music icon across the window and into the left-hand Folders view pane, and point at the Bank Correspondence folder. When Bank Correspondence becomes highlighted, release the right mouse button. (If you struggle with this, release the right mouse button at any time and abort the manoeuvre by clicking Cancel on the pop-up menu.)*

Copy Here

A pop-up menu now appears. Point at Copy Here and click once (back to the left button again). The Sample Music folder and all its contents is now copied to the Bank Correspondence folder. Feel free to check. Note that you can perform exactly the same move with individual files instead of folders.

Working with the Folder view can be fiddly so here's an alternative way to drag-and-drop files and folders. Try it and see – and, if it doesn't suit, just reverse the change you make in Step 1.

My Documents icon

Tools

Folder Options

Open each folder in its own window

Apply   OK

Until now we have been opening folders within a single My Documents window. Making this simple change has an interesting result that we'll see in the next step. Click the circle next to Open each folder in its own window to check that option, and then click Apply and OK.

My Music icon

Now double-click the My Music icon in the My Documents folder. As you can see, the folder opens in a brand new window. If necessary, click-and-drag the My Music window into a new position until you can see both its contents and My Documents at the same time (skip back to page 31 for help with moving windows). Our goal here is to move the letter file out of My Music and into My Pictures. So …

Letter to bank manager requesting a loan icon

Right-click the icon, hold down the mouse button and drag the file icon into the My Documents window. Point at the My Pictures icon and, when it becomes highlighted, release the mouse button.

Move Here

This time, click Move Here on the pop-up menu. The letter file disappears from the My Music folder and now lives in My Pictures. To finish, close both of the open windows. Just to be clear here: copying a file to a new location does not affect the original file – you simply end up with two exact copies of the same file in different folders. When you move a file, the original is permanently removed from its original location.

Copying multiple files

We've been working with single files and folders here but you can copy or move several all at the same time. You just have to make sure that they are all selected before you begin the operation.

To select multiple files and sub-folders within a folder, open the folder in My Documents, switch to List view (see page 71), hold down the Ctrl key, and click each target file or sub-folder in turn

To select all files and sub-folders within a folder, click the first file or sub-folder on the list, hold down the Shift key, and click the last file or sub-folder.

Now the selected files behave like a single unit. Try copying or moving them using one of the methods described above. When dragging-and-dropping, simply click on any one file or folder within the selected group and the whole lot will move as one, a little like a stack of playing cards in Solitaire.

Backing up folders

As you use your computer more and more, it becomes increasingly sensible to back up your files and folders regularly. Backing up simply involves making a copy of a file and storing it somewhere safe (i.e. not on your computer). Although hard disk failure is mercifully rare, it does happen – as, of course, does computer theft. Imagine all your work suddenly disappears out the door? It doesn't take a great leap of the imagination to understand the importance of backing up.

Moreover, you only really need to back up those files that you create yourself, as your programs – and even Windows – can always be reinstalled from scratch. This is why it helps to store your files within the My Documents folder: to backup everything at a stroke, simply copy My Documents to your CD-RW drive. We'll talk about using this drive in the next chapter.

A good backup regime takes no time at all and, thanks to the popularity of CD-RW drives, you can store a huge quantity of files (or a few huge files) on a single blank CD. However, you can also 'shrink' your files in order to squeeze even more of them onto a disc. It's a process known as *zipping*.

Select multiple files within a folder using either the Ctrl or Shift key methods described above. With your target files selected, right-click one of them (it doesn't matter which), select Send To on the pop-up menu, and then click on Compressed (zipped) Folder. This creates a new folder containing a copy of all the selected files.

What's remarkable here is that the new folder is actually smaller (in terms of data size) than the sum of the files within it. You can now copy or move the compressed folder to a floppy disk or CD-R/RW disc, thus saving space on your backup media. If you copy the compressed folder, remember to delete it from your hard disk when the backup is complete.

Incidentally, the compressed folder automatically assumes the title of one of the files within it. This isn't necessarily very helpful, but you can easily rename it. Flick back to page 64 to see how.

QUICK Q & A

How do I permanently empty the Recycle Bin?
Well, if you're sure you'll never need those deleted files again, right-click the Recycle Bin's Desktop icon and select Empty Recycle Bin from the pop-up menu.

PART 3 Working with drives

Earlier, we discussed drives in the context of hardware. Now let's put them to work. We'll assume here that your computer has four drives: a hard disk drive (that's a definite), a floppy drive (virtually certain), a CD-RW drive (highly likely) and a DVD-ROM drive (probable).

Using My Computer

On the Desktop, you'll find an icon for My Computer. Double-click it now.

 My Computer icon

Here we see our four drives. Note that each is assigned a drive letter (appended with a colon). This is how Windows tells one drive from another. In this case, we have:

- Floppy disk drive – A:
- Hard disk drive (labelled Local Disk) – C:
- DVD drive – D:
- CD-RW drive – E:

Now, the floppy drive is always A: and the hard disk drive always C:, but your CD-RW and DVD drives might be labelled the other way round depending upon how your system has been set up. It matters not: just bear in mind that each drive has its own, unique letter.

To see the files and folders stored on a drive, double-click its icon in My Computer. If there is no floppy, CD or DVD in the drive, Windows will return an error message; otherwise, you can view and open its contents (*see right*).

Hard disk drive. Of all the drives, the hard disk is by far the most important. Essentially, it 'is' your computer – home to Windows, programs and files. You *read data from* the hard disk drive every time you launch a program or perform a task; and you *save data* to the hard disk drive whenever you save a file. Just as with the My Documents window, you can use the View menu to work with files in different ways (*see below*). In fact, you can get to your files and folders using either My Documents or My Computer; they are entirely complementary.

My Computer takes you to your files and folders just as surely as My Documents – indeed, they are just different faces of the Windows Explorer.

Floppy disk drive. This venerable old stalwart has been threatened with extinction for years but still finds a place in most computers. The drive uses a portable form of media called a floppy disk – a hard plastic square that contains a magnetic disk capable of storing a maximum of 1.44 *Megabytes* of data. Floppies are most useful for transferring small amounts of data from one computer to another and, occasionally, for installing very small programs or drivers.

The underside of a floppy disk.

To use, simply insert a floppy disk into the slot on the drive. Push the disk fully home and be sure to put it in the right way up: the *bottom* of the disk has a visible metal circle.

Now you can copy or move files to the floppy disk using any of the methods described on page 74. Here is a worked example. First, pop a blank floppy disk in its drive.

 My Computer icon   *My Documents icon*

 A: icon   *Home Finance icon*

and   *Bank Correspondence icon*

This opens two windows: one showing the contents of the floppy disk (which is currently empty) and the other showing the now-familiar My Documents folder and its sub-folders. Arrange the windows on the Desktop so that you can see both at the same time (click-and-drag a Title Bar to move a window) and, using the right-click-and-hold manoeuvre described on pages 72-75, drag-and-drop a copy of the bank manager letter from Bank Correspondence into the A: window. The floppy disk now contains a copy of the letter. You can, of course, copy or move files from the floppy disk to any folder on the hard disk in just the same manner.

*To remove a floppy disk from its drive, always wait for the **drive activity light** to go out first. Act too soon and you could lose your data and/or damage the disk. When the light goes out, push the button next to the slot and out pops the disk.*

You can now 'write-protect' your floppy disk to ensure that its files cannot be accidentally deleted or overwritten. On the underneath of a disk, look for a tiny sliding mechanism. Move it to the open position (i.e. so that there's a hole in the disk) to write-protect the disk and safeguard your files. If you close the slider, the disk can be overwritten with fresh data.

There's not much else to say except to keep your floppies away from heat, direct sunlight and strong magnetic sources. Oh, and never, *ever* use a floppy to store truly critical files – they are simply not reliable enough.

CD-RW drive. We'll look at installing software from a CD-ROM disc on page 84 but for now let's take advantage of Windows XP's built-in *CD burning* capability. This lets you treat a recordable (or rewriteable) CD just like a floppy disk – but one with about 500 times the capacity for file storage.

Note: in this exercise, change E: to the drive letter that corresponds to your CD-RW drive.

 My Computer icon

 E: icon

Properties

Recording

Enable CD recording on this drive

Apply

OK

Here, we are simply setting up the drive to act as a CD recorder. This option, located in the Advanced tab of the Properties menu, may already be enabled on your computer but, if not, check it here.

Take no action

OK

Now pop a blank CD-R disc in the CD-RW drive. Push the button on the drive to open the tray, lay the disc flat on the tray printed- or label-side up (plain silver-side down), and push the button to close the tray. Windows will recognise what's happening and ask for instructions. Click Take no action and close the pop-up window by clicking OK.

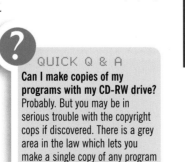

QUICK Q & A

Can I make copies of my programs with my CD-RW drive? Probably. But you may be in serious trouble with the copyright cops if discovered. There is a grey area in the law which lets you make a single copy of any program specifically and exclusively for backup purposes but, if in doubt, just hang on to the original installation disc and don't risk any accusation of piracy.

My Documents icon

 My Pictures icon

 Copy this folder

 E:

Copy

*Open My Documents and select the My Pictures folder
with a click. Now click Copy this folder option in the left
pane. In the pop-up window, select the CD-RW drive (E:)
and click Copy. What we're doing here is copying the
entire contents of My Pictures to the CD-R disc. You
could equally drag-and-drop the files as described earlier.*

*Now, for reasons too complicated to dwell upon, it is not
in fact possible for Windows to copy files directly to a
CD-R disc without a further step. The target files are
copied on the fly to a holding, or 'staging', area. This
gives you a chance to select more files to burn to the CD
later: just keep copying them to the drive as in Step 3.
In the meantime, when you click the Copy button, up
pops a bubble inviting you to burn the files straight
away. Ignore this and wait for it to disappear. Next time
around, you could click the bubble to take a shortcut to
Step 5 but let's go the long way around here.*

 E: icon

 Write these files to CD

 Copied Pictures

 Next

*Close My Documents, open My Computer and double-
click the E: icon. Now you can see the files and folders
awaiting burning in the main window pane – in this
case, My Pictures. Click Write these files to CD option
in the left pane. In the pop-up window, give the CD a
meaningful name – Copied Pictures, for example – and
click Next.*

Finish

*Windows now goes to work and burns the files onto the
CD-R disc. When the process completes, click the
Finish button. Now that the files have been copied, you
can read them in this or any other computer's CD-
ROM, CD-RW or DVD drive.*

*You can add more files to a CD-R disc in several
different burning 'sessions' until it is full. However, each
session wastes around 14MB of storage space – it's an
unavoidable overhead – so it's better to add files to the
staging area as you go along (see Step 4 above) and
then burn the lot in a single session (Step 5).*

You can also burn files onto a CD-RW disc time and time again whereas, once full, a CD-R disc cannot be used for recording again. Indeed, My Computer provides a quick way to completely clean a CD-RW disc – very useful if you want to start afresh.

DVD-ROM drive. As we remarked earlier, recordable DVD drives are not quite standard equipment on new computers yet. This means that you will typically use your DVD-ROM drive in one of three ways:

● To read CD-ROM, CD-R and CD-RW discs

● To install or run programs

● To watch DVD movies

Nothing too exciting there. In the first case, a DVD-ROM drive simply doubles-up as a spare CD-ROM drive; in the second, it comes into its own for installing huge programs that would otherwise fill several CD-ROMs; and in the third, you need to have a software movie player program installed on your computer.

Why buy a standalone DVD player when you can gather the family around your computer to watch a movie?

PART Working with programs

So far, we've worked exclusively with and within Windows. However, for all its games, features and built-in mini-programs like WordPad and Paint, remember that Windows is 'only' an operating system for your computer. To make the most of your hardware, you'll need some application software proper. In fact, your computer supplier almost certainly supplied a program or two as part of the deal.

Now, we can't begin to cover the ins and outs of all the different programs out there but we can show you a standard software installation and removal procedure.

Installing a program

To install a program means to copy its files from a CD-ROM or DVD-ROM to your computer's hard disk drive so you can use the program whenever you like without further recourse to the disc. However, some really weighty programs, particularly encyclopaedias, do keep a lot of the *multimedia* material on the disc as an alternative to clogging up your hard disk with large files that you seldom need. In such cases, you must keep the disc in the drive while the program is running.

We're going to install Microsoft Works Suite 2002 in this example – a collection of programs that includes Word, the popular word processor.

QUICK Q & A

Should I always buy a DVD-ROM version of a new program instead of CD-ROM?
Yes, providing it's no more expensive and your computer has a DVD drive. Thanks to DVD's greater capacity, it should save you shuffling between multiple CD-ROMs while you work or play.

Close any programs currently running on your computer and pop the program's installation disc in the CD-RW drive (if it's a CD-ROM) or DVD-ROM drive (if it's a DVD). The installation program should start automatically after a few seconds. In this case, we have a choice of how to proceed. We'd suggest that you always plump for the 'typical' option. Alternatively . . .

Microsoft Works Suite 2002 Setup

Microsoft

WORKS SUITE 2002 SETUP

Welcome!
The Installation Wizard will guide you through the process of installing Microsoft Works Suite 2002 onto your computer. Select the type of installation you want.

Typical — Automatically installs all Microsoft Works Suite 2002 programs with their standard components. Recommended for most users.

Minimum — Automatically installs all Microsoft Works Suite 2002 programs with a minimum number of components.

Custom — Installs only the Microsoft Works Suite 2002 programs you want.

Exit Setup

My Computer icon

D: icon

setup icon

If, however, nothing happens when you insert the disc, first ensure that you've put it into the drive the right way up (i.e. label up, shiny-side down). If there's still no action, open My Computer, double-click the icon for the drive that contains the disc (D: here), switch to List view (see page 71), and look for a file named setup. Double-click it to kick-start the installation. Alternatively . . .

Start

Control Panel

Add or Remove Programs icon

Add New Programs

CD or Floppy

Next

Finish

This is another alternative to try if the installation procedure does not begin automatically. Windows searches your floppy and CD/DVD drives for the necessary files and launches installation itself. Again, be sure that the disc is already in its drive.

Start

All Programs

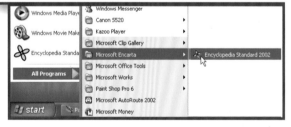

Generally, you can sit back and do nothing during installation, but some programs ask you where you want the files to be saved or let you pick and choose between optional components. Just accept the default suggestions every time.

When the installation process completes, you may have to restart your computer. Now click Start and look for your new software in the All Programs menu. New programs are highlighted in the menu. You launch the program with a click from here, first expanding any sub-menus if necessary.

I Agree

*If you are presented with a **user licence** when you first run a program, read the terms and conditions carefully (you'll discover that you're not allowed to make copies and flog them at a car boot sale, for example) and click Agree or Accept. If you disagree or refuse to accept its terms, the program will not run.*

Product key

In this example, we are also prompted for the product key the first time we run Word. Also known as a security code or serial number, this ostensibly guarantees that you own a legitimate copy of the program (rather then one bought at a car boot sale). The code will be printed on the CD/DVD box or in the manual or on a paper insert in the box, or somewhere. Enter the code exactly as you see it, respecting the use of upper and lower case, dashes and spaces. You may also be invited to register the program with the developer in order to receive free updates and upgrades. This can normally be done over the internet, so perhaps wait until the next section!
*NB. Word comes with Microsoft's **Product Activation** feature, just like Windows XP (see Glossary).*

Uninstalling a program

There will come a time when you no longer have a need for one or more of your programs. Now, it generally does no harm to let redundant software rest undisturbed on your hard disk. However, hard disks have a finite capacity and even today, when they routinely top 60 **Gigabytes**, you may eventually need to free up space to install some new programs. Or you may install a program that you simply don't get along with.

Once uninstalled, a program can no longer be run on your computer. You can always *re*install it, of course, providing you still have the original CD-ROM or DVD.

One point to note: uninstalling a program does not *usually* remove any files that you created yourself with it. Uninstalling Word, for instance, will not delete your letter files. However, because programs often use proprietary file formats, you may find that you can no longer access your files without the original program. The moral of which is: take care, and use non-proprietary file formats wherever possible.

QUICK Q & A
Q: Why are software boxes so big and bulky when there's nothing inside but a CD-ROM and a lot of fresh air?
A: They look good on superstore shelves.

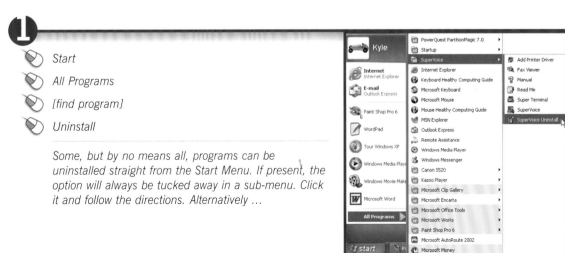

Start

All Programs

[find program]

Uninstall

Some, but by no means all, programs can be uninstalled straight from the Start Menu. If present, the option will always be tucked away in a sub-menu. Click it and follow the directions. Alternatively …

Start

Control Panel

Add or Remove Programs icon

Change or Remove Programs

[select program]

Change/Remove

Yes

The Add or Remove Programs window shows you a list of all the software installed on your computer, and you simply highlight the target program and click the Change/Remove button. (If there are separate Change and Remove buttons, click Remove.) Confirm your intentions in the next window by clicking Yes.

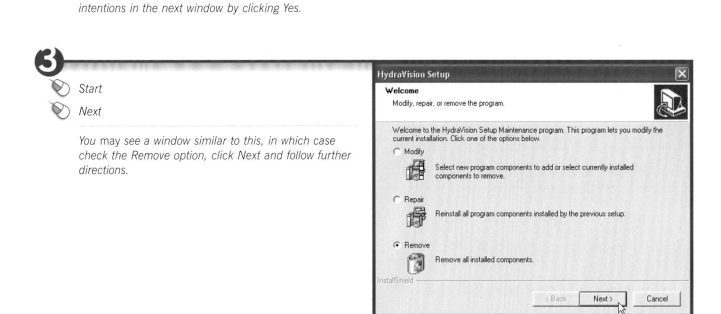

Start

Next

You may see a window similar to this, in which case check the Remove option, click Next and follow further directions.

QUICK Q & A

Q: I've just bought this expensive new program and I can't find the manual!
A: A sign of the times, we're afraid. Manuals are now routinely supplied in electronic form, which means there's a file somewhere on the installation disc. As often

as not, this will be an Adobe Acrobat file, which can only be opened and read with a program called Acrobat Reader. A copy of this will be provided on the disc along with the manual (or, if not, you can download it from www.adobe.com).

Unfreezing your computer

Windows is designed for multi-tasking (i.e. doing several things at once). This means that you can easily run two, three or more programs at the same time – perhaps an e-mail program, a web browser, a word processor and a music player.

However, there are certain limitations. Without getting too technical, the number of programs and tasks you can perform simultaneously depends on how much memory your computer has and, to a lesser extent, the speed of its processor. If you try to do *too* much, everything will slow to a crawl and you'll spend more time drumming your fingers on your desk waiting for windows to open than typing on your keyboard. In the worst case, your computer may actually 'freeze'. No matter what you click, nothing happens: the screen display refuses to change and your computer is effectively lifeless. What to do?

Well, you have two options. First, press and hold the Ctrl + Alt + Delete keys on your keyboard simultaneously. This launches a window called Windows Task Manager. As soon as it appears, release all three keys.

Task Manager has several tabs but you're interested in Applications. Here you'll see a list of all programs currently running on your computer. If any program is marked as 'Not Responding' in the Status, that's your culprit right there. Select the program and click End Task. Windows will now close this – *and only this* – program, and you should be able to use your computer as normal again. The downside is that any open file within that program will also close, and so you'll lose the changes you made since the last time you saved it. We'll come to that in the very next section.

If Task Manager can't resolve your troubles and your computer is absolutely frozen, there is another option – but this one is strictly for Emergency Use Only. Press the reset button on the system unit. This bypasses the usual shutdown procedure and immediately turns your computer off and on again. Here, too, you'll lose any unsaved files, and this time it affects *all* open programs. Windows may also launch a **diagnostic utility** before it restarts.

There's no need to panic if a program freezes your computer – Task Manager can usually save the day.

The reset button really is the last resort.

Save your work-in-progress with a button, a menu command or a keyboard shortcut.

The all-important Save button

If there's one lesson that all computer owners learn the hard way, it is this: losing your work is a nightmare. Be it a power failure, a system freeze or an accidental click on the wrong button, there's nothing like watching a critical file or project disappear forever to make you wish you'd never set eyes on your hardware.

But it needn't be so! Barring the most extreme misadventure, any file saved to your hard disk is safe. Back on page 65, we looked at how to save a new file using the Save As command. This same procedure applies in virtually all programs: you give each new file a name and save it. However, the critical thing – the really, *really* critical thing – is remembering to save your work *as you go along*.

When you first save a file, it is allocated a slice of hard disk space. However, the moment you open and change that file in any way – add or delete a word or a sentence or an image, or change the formatting, or do anything whatsoever – the open file and the saved file are no longer identical. The open file is held in a kind of flux while you work, and is vulnerable to all sorts of mishap. This is why it is vital to save your work continually. The idea is simply to minimise the period between your last save and the moment catastrophe strikes – and, since you never know when catastrophe is going to strike, this means saving your work *frequently*. We would suggest that once every couple of minutes is a good target.

How do you save your work? In almost every case, you will find a Save button on your program's Toolbar (it often looks like a floppy disk). Failing this, click File on the Menu Bar and look for the Save command.

There are some exceptions, however. E-mail programs, for instance, automatically save incoming messages without the need for you to do anything.

Alternatively, many programs allow you to use a keyboard shortcut: pressing the Ctrl + S keys simultaneously has the same effect as clicking Save.

Every time you save a file, the file on your hard disk is overwritten with the open version. If you wish to avoid this, use the Save As command instead, and save the open file with a new name. Thus you might open your 'Letter to the bank manager requesting a loan' and save it immediately as, say, 'Loan agreement details'. Now you can use the original file as a useful template without in any way affecting it.

What does what?

The range of programs is truly vast, from free utilities to super-expensive video editing suites. Moreover, while you probably know a few of the big software names, like Microsoft, there is tremendous competition in most markets. We would strongly advise that you research any potential purchase thoroughly, as no two programs are ever quite identical. What might appear to be a minor weakness in one slightly cheaper program may, in fact, make it wholly unsuitable for your intentions; on the other hand, you can often save a good deal of money by opting for software that has a lower specification but still does all you need of it.

There is also a tremendous degree of cross-over among genres. A word processor, for instance, is perfect for writing letters (and computer manuals) but can also handle figures and even basic design and illustrative work. Don't splash out on new software if your existing programs can handle your needs.

Each new program involves another learning curve. However, Windows encourages a roughly standard interface, or appearance, so it's often possible to work out the basics fairly quickly.

These screens show very different types of program – one is designed for editing text; the other for editing images – but note the similarities. Both have a Title Bar, a Menu Bar, a number of Toolbars and a large central working area. In short, you click things – buttons, menus, icons – to make stuff happen.

QUICK Q & A

When a program asks me if I want to read the ReadMe file, what does it mean?
A ReadMe file is a text document on a program's installation disc that contains important or late-breaking news concerning the program. For instance, if a bug has been discovered since the CD-ROM was pressed, or if there is a misprint in the manual, you may find details in the ReadMe file. It might also provide help and instructions with the program installation. So, yes – always read the ReadMe.

Most Windows programs have a broadly similar appearance regardless of what they actually do.

Here is a very rough, ready and by no means exhaustive
guide to popular types of program and what they do
best:

Program type	What can you do with it?
Antivirus	Prevent potentially harmful viruses from damaging your computer.
CAD (Computer Aided Design)	Design products digitally on a computer.
CD burning	Record audio, video and data compilations onto CDs.
Database	Collate and manage complex and/or large quantities of data.
DTP (Desktop Publishing)	Design documents and projects using text and images.
E-mail	Send, receive and manage e-mail messages.
Financial management	Keep tabs on your incomings and outgoings.
Firewall	Protect your computer from internet *hackers*.
Games	Computer games range from child-friendly educational tools to blood-thirsty shoot-'em-ups.
Image editor	Edit and enhance digital pictures imported from a scanner or a digital camera.
Instant messenger	Exchange text messages across the internet in real time.
Multimedia player	Play music and videos on your computer.
Office suite	A compendium of business tools, typically including a word processor, spreadsheet, database, e-mail and PIM.
PIM (Personal Information Manager)	Keep track of your contacts with an address book, diary and calendar.
Presentation	Create professional presentations, particularly suited to sales proposals.
Project management	Control a complex project from conception to completion.
Reference	General and specific research – dictionary, encyclopaedia, atlas, etc.
Sound editor	Record and edit digital sound files, including musical instruments.
Speech recognition	Train your computer to recognise your voice (well, up to a point).
Spreadsheet	Perform advanced calculations with figures laid out in rows and columns.
System utilities	Maintain and trouble-shoot your computer at a sub-Windows level.
Video editor	Turn raw camcorder footage into a polished movie.
Web browser	Visit web pages and sites on the internet.
Web editor	Design and build your own web pages.
Word processor	Create and edit text-based documents.

PART **4** # The internet

E-mail, websites, ***online shopping***, *instant chat*, community groups, research, ***online gaming***, ***file-sharing***, live news and entertainment updates, ***streaming*** video and radio … all this and much, much more is possible with your computer. In fact, there's every chance that you bought a computer precisely because you want to be part of this global communications network called the internet.

In this section, we will discuss how to get online in the first place and then spend a little time looking at using a web browser and an e-mail program. We'll also practise downloading a file, and round up with a touch of essential paranoia.

PART **Getting online**

To start using the internet, you need four things: a computer, a modem, a telephone line and an account with an Internet Service Provider (ISP). The first you already have, the second is built right into it (probably – if not, you can always get an external, standalone modem), and the third we will take for granted. What, then, is an ISP?

Connection to the internet

ISP

Your computer

To access the internet you need an account with an Internet Service Provider.

Access for all

The internet is essentially a network of connected computers. Many are just like yours, others act as storage facilities for large amounts of data, and still others control the flow of information through and around the network. However, you can't tap into the internet directly: rather, you must enlist the services of an ISP. Your computer uses a *modem* and the telephone line to connect to a computer at your ISP's premises, and it this computer that links you to the internet at large.

Now, there are two distinct flavours of ISP. Most offer a straightforward connection to the internet and throw in a few welcome extras like e-mail accounts, free *web space* and perhaps a bunch of promotional incentives. Others, notably America Online (AOL), are properly called Online Services Providers, as they offer a range of exclusive member-only services – online chat, shopping, *parental controls* and the like – of which internet access is only one. However, while AOL is often justly regarded as being particularly suitable for newcomers to the internet, it does require you to install and use proprietary software. For this reason more than any other, we're going to show you how to connect to a 'standard' ISP using nothing but the tools built right into Windows.

Broadband-in-a-box lets you supercharge your internet connection without an engineer.

Picking an ISP

There is certainly no such thing as the 'perfect' ISP, and in fact it's remarkably difficult to find two companies offering precisely the same deal at the same time. This makes like-for-like comparisons all the trickier. However, here are the major factors to take into consideration:

Cost. These days, most ISPs push you towards paying a regular monthly subscription, for which you get more or less unlimited access to the internet and no telephone charges. However, if you only connect to the internet very occasionally, you may save money by opting for a 'Pay As You Go' service, whereby you pay local telephone rates per minute spent online.

Technical support. You may well need occasional help with your internet service so check whether potential ISPs offer free telephone support, even if only for an introductory period, or whether they charge the earth with premium rate telephone numbers.

E-mail. How many e-mail accounts will you get? One may suffice but you may prefer that every member of the family has a unique e-mail address, especially if you set up User Accounts (discussed in Appendix 3).

How unlimited is unlimited? Despite claims that a monthly fee buys you the freedom to stay online for as long as you like, many ISPs operate irritating cut-off schemes. You may temporarily lose the internet connection after any continuous period of two hours or if you leave the connection unattended (i.e. you stop actively *surfing*) for more than ten minutes or so. Check the Terms and Conditions carefully.

Broadband?

Broadband internet service differs from *dial-up* (a modem using the telephone line) in four ways. It is around ten times faster, so web pages load more quickly and you can send and receive large files with ease. There are no telephone charges to pay, just a fixed monthly subscription fee. You can use the telephone *while your computer is online*, which isn't possible with a dial-up connection unless you have a separate phone line reserved for internet access. And the connection is '**always-on**' – i.e. your computer has a fixed, permanent hotline to your ISP.

There are also various different types of broadband internet access around, including *cable*, *DSL* and *satellite*. Where you live has a large bearing on which broadband service, if any, you can actually get.

Is broadband worth getting? Our answer is a definite yes – providing you can justify the extra expense. A broadband connection means that the internet is 'just there', a mere click away at any time. This is how it should be! Moreover, the recent introduction of DIY broadband kits has made broadband easy to set up without the need for an engineer.

	Maximum (theoretical) connection speed	Minimum time to download one Megabyte of data	Maximum data that can be downloaded per minute
Dial-up connection (modem plus telephone line)	56,000 *bits* per second	2 minutes 30 seconds	0.4MB
Cable or DSL broadband	512,000 bits per second*	16.4 seconds	3.66MB

*NB This is the current entry-level broadband speed operating in the UK. Considerably faster broadband connections are also available – for a considerable premium.

Details you need

We'll assume that you've picked an ISP and plan to take your first steps online with a dial-up service rather than broadband. It's likely that the ISP will provide all you need on a CD-ROM – just pop it in the drive, follow the instructions and you'll be online in minutes. Here, however, we'll go it alone and set up a connection manually. This way, you'll understand a little more about the process *and* be able to transfer your dial-up account to any other computer without relying on ISP-supplied software.

All you need to get started are these three things:

User name. This is the name you'll use to log in to your ISP when you go online. It will also form your e-mail address: e.g. yourname@yourisp.com. You may well find that somebody has already signed up with your name, however – especially if you're called Bob Smith – so do think up an alternative or two.

Password. This ensures that you and you alone can access your internet account and collect your e-mail. A random combination of letters and figures makes for a safer password than the name of your dog.

Access telephone number. This is the telephone number that your computer modem will dial to get online. And yes, engaged tones are perfectly possible.

You can usually agree these details in advance with your ISP over the telephone. Or, if you opt to use the ISP's CD-ROM, you'll be prompted to enter a user name and password during the sign-up procedure.

Making the connection

The very first thing you must do, of course, is connect your modem to a telephone socket. Dig out the modem cable that came with your computer system. One end plugs into the 'line' socket on the modem and the other into a standard telephone socket. If there are two sockets on the modem, the second is for connecting a telephone handset, and should be clearly marked or labelled as such. Check the computer or modem manual if in doubt. Do remember that you cannot use the telephone while your computer is connected to the internet. Callers will get an engaged tone.

My Network Places icon

 View network connections

 Create a new connection

 Next

My Network Places is an icon on your Desktop. Look for the network connections options in the left pane. This process launches the New Connection Wizard.

 Connect to the internet

 Next

 Set up my connection manually

 Next

 Connect using a dial-up modem

 Next

Here, you simply make selections from the Wizard's suggestions and keep clicking the Next button.

 [ISP name]

 Next

Type in the name of your ISP. In this case, it happens to be Freeserve.

 [ISP access telephone number]

 Next

This is the number that your modem will dial to connect to your ISP. Don't use spaces.

[user name]

 [password]

 [confirm password]

 Next

Enter your user name exactly as agreed with your ISP.
Here you also type in your chosen password, twice.
Note that the password itself is masked on screen so no
snoops peering over your shoulder can see it. Ensure
that the three options are all checked and click Next
again.

 Add a shortcut to this connection to my desktop

 Finish

Tick the shortcut box and click Finish. That's it – you're
now ready to go online for the first time.

 Dial

As the Wizard closes, you should find that a Connect
window pops up. Click Dial and your modem will
attempt to connect to your ISP. Expect to hear a series
of shrieks from your modem. This is quite normal!

When the modem makes a successful connection to
your ISP, an all-important icon appears in the
Notification Area on the Taskbar (see page 57). This is
the sign (the only sign, in fact, aside from a temporary
balloon) that you are now online.

 ISP Status icon

Disconnect

To disconnect from the internet at any time, double-
click this Taskbar icon to launch the Status window.
This tells you how long you've been online, your
connection speed, and how much data your modem
has sent and received. Click the Disconnect button to
make your modem 'hang up'. You are now no longer
online, and the Taskbar icon disappears.

 ISP icon

To reconnect, look for the new ISP icon on your Desktop
and double-click it. This launches the same window we
saw in Step 7. Click the Dial button as before.
Always remember to disconnect (as in Step 10) **when
you have finished your internet session!**

PART 4 Browsing the web

OK, so now you can get your computer online with an ISP account. It's time to start exploring the web. We should stress that the web is only one part of the internet but, to be honest, it's the fun part. Once you've mastered a few browser basics, you can visit any web page or website in the world.

Internet Explorer

A browser is a computer program designed for viewing web pages. Some web pages are little more than a few words of text on a plain background; others are fearsomely interactive, multimedia, full bells-and-whistles affairs. A web*site* is any self-contained but interlinked collection of web pages.

When you type a web page address into a browser, the browser sends a request across the internet to the computer responsible for storing that particular page. If the request is successful, and it usually is, a copy of the page is sent to the browser. That is, the browser **downloads** a copy of the web page onto your computer. What you have to bear in mind here is a simple equation: large web pages take longer to download than small pages because more data has to be transferred across the internet. Large pages tend to have lots of pictures or sounds or animations (or whatever); small pages are mainly text.

Web pages download in fits and starts, with the result that they 'load' in your browser piece by piece. The text may appear first, followed by the images, or vice versa. To see a web page in all its glory, you have to wait for the download to complete.

We're going to work with Internet Explorer in this example, partly because it comes free with Windows and partly because it's overwhelmingly the most popular browser around.

You should find an icon right on your Desktop: double-click this to launch the program. Failing that, there's a link to Internet Explorer on the pinned programs section of the Start Menu (see page 58).

When you double-click the Desktop icon or click its entry in the Start Menu, Internet Explorer generates a Dial-up Connection

window (*See above left*). Click Connect and the program will dial up your ISP. Moreover, if you put a tick in the Connect automatically box, Internet Explorer will in future dial your ISP as soon as it launches without bothering to ask.

If, however, you manually connect to your ISP *before* launching Internet Explorer – as described in the previous section – this window will not appear for the simple reason that the internet connection has already been made. In short, you have a choice: either manually connect to the internet before firing up your browser (or, as we shall see, e-mail program), or let the program do the work.

As soon as Internet Explorer starts, close it again by clicking the red cross in the top right corner of the window. This time, you should see a message similar to the screenshot above right.

Click Disconnect Now and Internet Explorer will automatically disconnect you from your ISP; click Stay Connected and you will stay online even though Internet Explorer itself is no longer running. This would be useful if, for example, you were finished browsing but still had e-mail to check. Alternatively, put a tick in the Don't use Auto Disconnect box and you won't see this message again. You must now remember to close the connection manually every time you wish to end your internet session, as shown in Step 10 on page 99.

Remember, if you're ever in any doubt about whether your computer is currently online (connected to the internet) or offline (not), look for the 'connected computers' icon next to or near the Taskbar clock. If it's there, you're definitely online!

Browser basics

When you launch Internet Explorer, it should look something like this. Here is a key to all the relevant features.

Menu Bar Click any of the titles here to see a dropdown menu. See page 102 for more details.

Title Bar This displays the title of the web page currently open in the browser. Note the standard minimise window, maximise window and close program buttons at the far right.

Flag This useful icon tells you when Internet Explorer is active and when it's at rest. If the flag is waving, you know that the browser is busy downloading a web page; when it's static, the download is finished and the page should appear complete in the main window. Your browser may not have a flag icon at all, incidentally: ISPs love to install their own icons here, which is one of the unavoidable consequences of using an ISP-supplied CD-ROM to set up your account.

Toolbar Lots of useful buttons. See page 102 for more details.

Address Bar Action stations! This is where you type the 'address' of a web page in the address box and either press the Enter key or click the Go button at the right end of the Address Bar. Using Enter is usually quicker since your hands are on the keyboard anyway. Every web page has a unique address.

Status Bar Like the flag icon, this tells you about your browser's current activity. The progress bar fills up gradually as a page is downloaded. When it becomes solid green, the page is complete and the bar disappears. More importantly, if you see a yellow padlock, it means the page is *secure* (e.g. on an online shopping website, your credit card details will be safely encrypted).

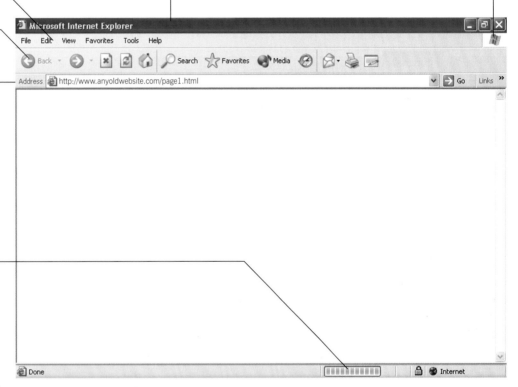

Understanding web addresses

http:// *Hypertext Transfer Protocol, essentially a standard that lets browsers make sense of web pages. You can leave 'http://' out of most web addresses, as Internet Explorer adds it automatically, but only when the next part of the address begins with 'www'.*

www *World Wide Web. The part of the internet concerned with web pages and sites (as opposed to the part concerned with e-mail or newsgroups).*

anyoldwebsite *The domain. This is simply the name of the parent website.*

.com *The suffix. There are lots of these, but '.com' (for company, originally) is the most popular. Country-specific suffixes include '.co.uk' for UK-based companies.*

/ *A forward slash indicates that the next part of the address is a sub-division of the domain, just like a file within a folder.*

page1 *The title of a specific web page. It may have a name, a number or even a bunch of typographical symbols.*

.html *As with the files you create on your computer, web pages have file formats and extensions. HTML – Hypertext Markup Language, with the extension '.html' or '.htm' – is by far the most common language used to design web pages.*

File *Includes the Print Preview function that shows you what a web page will look like on paper before you commit to printing it. You, might, for instance, change the paper layout from portrait to landscape when printing a wide web page (web pages do not have fixed dimensions – they can be as long or as wide as a web designer cares to make them).*

View *If you have difficulty reading tiny text on web pages, use the Text Size command to increase the text from Medium to Larger or Largest. You can also use the Full Screen option to temporarily hide the Toolbars and enlarge a web page to fill the entire screen – a handy feature that reduces the need to scroll.*

Tools *This is where you can configure your browser to the nth degree. In truth, there's little here to worry about, but it is worth checking one setting. Click Tools, then Internet Options, and look in the Connections tab. Your ISP should appear in the main box, and the 'Always dial my default connection' box should be checked. If you were now to select the 'Never dial a connection option', Internet Explorer would stop trying to go online when you launch it. This would be the right choice if you have opted for making manual connections to your ISP, as discussed on page 100.*

Help *Self-evidently, this is where you would seek assistance with your browser. Click Help, then Contents and Index, move to the Index tab, and search for help on any keyword. Try Tip of the Day too, and learn all manner of browser shortcuts. For instance, you can create buttons on a special Links Toolbar for all your favourite web pages.*

Edit *Includes a useful Find command. Type in a keyword, click Find Next and the word you are looking for will be highlighted on the current web page (if present).*

Favorites *Very important, this one! The Favorites menu is where you store links (called 'bookmarks') to web pages that you wish to return to some other time. There will already be a few entries in your Favorites menu but you can add your own links at will. How? We'll cover that on pages 105-106.*

Print *Click this and the page you're currently viewing will pop straight out of your printer. That's the theory; in practice, web pages have a habit of printing peculiarly so we'd suggest that you use Print Preview first.*

Discuss *Sorry, we've never been able to make this one do anything useful, so we invite you to ignore it completely.*

Back *Surfing is largely a matter of following links – Page A leads to Page B, which takes you to Page C and so forth – and it's very easy to lose track of your starting point. Clicking this button takes you back to the last page you viewed (i.e. click Back while viewing Page C and Page B will reopen).*

Forward. *If, however, you backtrack too far, this button lets you skip forward again, page by page.*

Home *When you launch Internet Explorer, it opens your 'home page'. This might be a Microsoft page, or your ISP's website or any other page. If you tend to visit the same page regularly, why not make this your home page instead? To do this, go online, open the desired web page in your browser, and then do this:*

 Tools

 Internet Options

 General tab

 Use Current

 Apply

 OK

Wherever you are on the web, one click on the Home button will take you straight to this home page.

Favorites *This button displays your bookmarks as clickable links in a special pane on the left side of the browser window – a nice, easy way to work with bookmarks that saves you having to open the Favorites menu every time.*

Search *We're going to ignore this one for now, if you don't mind. We'll explain why on page 107.*

History *Internet Explorer remembers which web pages you visit. Click this button to see them in that left window pane again. You can view the list in different ways and even search for keywords – just experiment with the options at the top of the pane. If, however, you'd prefer your browser to forget your surfing history, perhaps for privacy reasons, do this:*

 Tools

 Internet Options

 General tab

 Clear History

 Yes

 OK

Microsoft Internet Explorer

File   Edit   View   Favorites   Tools   Help

Back • ⊙ • ✕ 🗘 🏠 🔍 Search ⭐ Favorites 🌐 Media ⊘ ✉ • 🖨 🗎

Stop *Some web pages take forever to appear in your browser, particularly if they are crammed with graphics. Other pages are just 'broken' and will never download properly, although your browser may not realise this. In either case, press Stop to, er, stop the page in its tracks. Note that you don't have to stop or wait for a page to finish before leaving it for another.*

Refresh *This button forces Internet Explorer to download a web page afresh. This is particularly useful with pages where the content changes regularly – news headlines, for instance, or live sports scores. Every time you press Refresh, you get the most up to date version of the page. It's also worth trying if a page fails to load properly the first time around (e.g. one or more pictures fail to appear or the text is all askance).*

Media *Internet Explorer can play certain kinds of audio and video clips without having to launch a separate program. When you click on a link to such a clip, the browser asks you if that's OK; if you say yes, the clip plays in a special pane to the left of the main window.*

Mail *This button simply fires up your default e-mail program, more of which shortly.*

Opening a web page

To open and view a web page, first go online. Now click once in the Address Bar box to position the blinking cursor ready for typing, and type in the address of the page you wish to see. Use lowercase. Press Enter or click the Go button and the page will download and appear in the browser's main window.

If you enter a domain name – something like www.anyoldwebsite.com – the browser will automatically open at the domain's home page, which is usually the best place to start. Otherwise, enter the full address (www.anyoldwebsite.com/page1.html) to go straight to a particular page.

When there is already an address in the box and you want to enter a new one, click on it once. This highlights the entire address. You can either clear it with the Delete key or simply overtype your new address.

Alternatively, position the blinking cursor at the end of the address and clear it with the Backspace key, or at the start and use Delete key. These are the basic skills you practised with WordPad.

If a page is too large for the browser window, scrollbars appear on the right side of the window and perhaps also along the bottom. Use these to navigate through the page. You can also move through a page by rotating the wheel on your mouse, or by using the arrow keys on your keyboard. You can even jump straight to the very top and bottom of a web page by pressing the Home and End keys respectively.

Hyperlinks

A hyperlink is a clickable link on any web page that takes you to any other web page. But how exactly do you recognise them? Well, a hyperlink can be a word, a phrase, an icon, a picture, or *part* of a picture, a box, a button or just about anything at all. The way you tell is by watching the mouse pointer: when it changes shape to a hand with a pointing finger, you've know you've found a hyperlink. Click once, and the browser will open the new page.

An important observation at this juncture. Generally, clicking a hyperlink replaces the current page with a new one. Sometimes, however, clicking a hyperlink opens *another* Internet Explorer window. You now have two Internet Explorers running, each displaying a different web page (*See opposite page*).

You can work with these windows independently – swap between them using the Taskbar buttons – or close either or both at any time. Clicking a hyperlink in either window may well spawn a third window, and so on and so on. It can get confusing but always remember that you can easily resize windows, close them, or minimise them to the Taskbar.

Hyperlinks can be hidden anywhere on a web page. Uncover them with the pointer.

Clicking a link often spawns a fresh browser window.

That old right-click comes in handy on the web.

In fact, you can force a hyperlink to open a new window whenever you like. This is particularly useful if you want to use one page as your base: each hyperlink opens a new page in its own window, leaving your original page open and unaffected. To do this, *right*-click a hyperlink and select Open in New Window from the pop-up menu (*See above right*), or hold down the Shift key when you click the link.

The web is vast and chaotic, and you *will* get lost. Indeed, that's part of the fun! Just remember to bookmark good pages as you go along, and use the History function to track down and revisit forgotten pages.

Oh yes, bookmarks …

QUICK Q & A

What's a cookie, and why do web pages keep sending them to my computer?
A cookie is a small text file saved on your computer's hard disk that contains preferences and other information about your use of a website. They are not harmful, and allow a website to, for instance, remember your name next time you visit (assuming that you provide this information in the first place), keep track of your purchases, or just tell how often you visit the site and how long you stay each time. Find out more, including how to stop or delete them, by searching on 'cookie' in Internet Explorer's Help menu.

Bookmarks

To 'bookmark' a web page is to save a link to it on your computer so that you can easily revisit it without ever again having to enter its address in the browser. Here's how.

 Favorites

 Add To Favorites

 [name of page]

OK

When you visit a web page that you'd like to return to, add it to the browser's Favorites menu. Click Favorites on the Menu Bar while the page is open, and select Add To Favorites. The Name box shows you the current title of the page but you can change this to something more memorable if you like. Click OK.

Favorites

  [bookmark]

Click Favorites again and you'll see a list of bookmarks in the dropdown menu. To revisit any bookmarked page, simply select it here and click.

  Favorites

  Organize Favorites

  Create Folder

  [name of the folder you wish to create]

To keep things tidy, you can create your own folders for bookmarks. Return to the Favorites menu, but this time click Organize Favorites. Here you can make new folders and name them to suit. You can also select bookmarks and move them to any specified folder with the Move to Folder button (or, indeed, you can drag-and-drop bookmarks straight to folders).

  Favorites

  Add To Favorites

  Create In

  [select folder]

  OK

Next time you come to bookmark a page, highlight the relevant folder before clicking OK and the bookmark will be saved within. If there's no suitable folder to hand, you can even make a fresh one at this point by clicking the New Folder button. Remember, you can also work with your bookmarks by clicking the Favorites button on the Toolbar (see page 103).

QUICK Q & A

Q: Tell me more about plug-ins.

A: Well, plug-ins, or 'ActiveX components', are free downloadable utilities that super-charge a browser's capabilities. Take Macromedia Flash, for instance. Flash is a coding language sometimes used to design and build entire websites (as an alternative to HTML). Now, if you try to view such a website, you'll be hit with a message that you need the Flash plug-in to proceed. This is unquestionably an irritant, particularly as you are unlikely to know whether or not the site is really worth viewing until you've seen it. The upside, however, is that you only need to download any plug-in once (until the developer releases an upgrade, that is). They generally download reasonably quickly and install semi-automatically.

Searching

To find information on the web, you often have to go looking for it, and this requires the services of a search engine. Search engines are complicated creatures but essentially they roam the web and compile a searchable index of all they find. This index is partial at best – the web is just too vast and in too great a state of flux to ever be pinned down completely – but it's usually sufficient to help you home in on your chosen subject.

There are many search engines around, and you are free to use whichever ones you fancy. Indeed, the reason we glossed over the Internet Explorer's Search button on page 103 is because it links to one particular search engine (operated, unsurprisingly, by a division of Microsoft), and this is rather misleading. We would recommend instead that you experiment with several search engines and bookmark your favourites.

At the time of writing, the most effective search engine *in most cases* is Google. It's also the simplest to use and sports the least fussy interface.

To test drive Google, enter the following web address in your browser's Address Bar – www.google.com – and press Enter or click Go. Now type a keyword or two in the search box, using lowercase, and click the Google Search button.

QUICK Q & A

What other search engines are there?
Oh, plenty. Try Yahoo! (www.yahoo.com), MSN (www.msn.com), AltaVista (www.altavista.com) and Lycos (www.lycos.com) for starters.

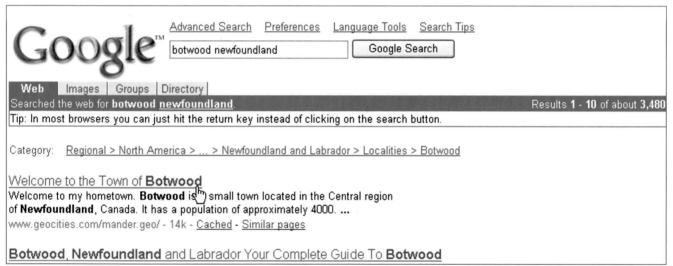

Google then searches through its index and returns a list of web pages that include your keywords.

These are ranked by relevance, which means that the pages at the top of the list are more likely to be what you're looking for than those at the bottom. Each '*hit*' is accompanied with a few lines of text to give the flavour of what the page is all about. Click any blue, underlined page title (i.e. hyperlink) to open that page in your browser.

Google is not infallible, of course – no search engine is – but it does work remarkably well. Two tips: use as many keywords as you can to narrow your searches and increase relevance; and enclose phrases within quotation marks to make Google look for that specific phrase and not just the keywords in any old order.

Downloads

Aside from viewing web pages, you may wish to use your browser to download files: an application form, perhaps, or a plug-in, or a video clip or sound file, or even a program. Downloading a file involves transferring a copy of it from some computer somewhere to your own computer's hard disk.

Let's try it out. For our example, we'll download a free music player called Winamp. This program may not be available forever, and the web pages we work with here may change appearance. However, the purpose of this example is to illustrate a fairly standard download procedure.

Internet Explorer icon

www.winamp.com [Enter]

[link]

Launch your browser and enter the web page address quoted above. The trick now is to find the hyperlink that leads to the download page. Winamp actually makes this easy – just click the big obvious picture – but sometimes you have to root around to find the right link.

Begin download

There are several versions of Winamp available but here we want the full version. It's over 3 Megabytes in size so this will take around 8–10 minutes to download with a modem. Click the link to proceed.

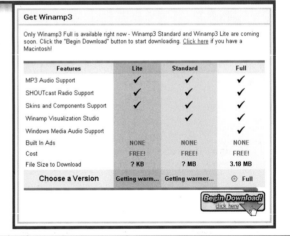

Save

Up pops a File Download window. Internet Explorer is asking what you want to do with the target file (i.e. the Winamp program). You want to save it to your hard disk, so click the Save button.

Desktop

 Save

Now you have to tell the browser where to save the file. We recommend that you use the Desktop – it's easy to find the file when the download is complete – so select Desktop from the dropdown Save in: box and click Save.

Make a cup of tea

Well, you can monitor the process of the download if you like, or you can go and do something more interesting. In any case, let Internet Explorer complete the download before you start any fresh work on your computer.

 Close

 winamp icon

When the download completes, click Close. Now close down Internet Explorer and come offline. On the Desktop you will find an icon representing the newly downloaded file. Double-click this now to launch the program installation.

I Agree

Next

Install

The rest is basically a case of following instructions. Installation procedures vary considerably so skip back to page 84 for an overview. However, the key thing here is that you've found a useful, free program on the internet and downloaded it to your computer. Well done!

PART **4** # E-mail

Away from the wonders of web pages, we find the internet's true 'killer application' – e-mail. Those of us who have been using e-mail for years now take it so much for granted that even a temporary blip in the service can induce panic ('I can't live without my Inbox!'); those who come to it anew are soon swayed by e-mail's immediacy and, dare we say it, simplicity.

There are free web-based e-mail services available, like Hotmail, so it is in fact possible to send and receive messages using only Internet Explorer. However, we're going to use the specialist e-mail software that comes with Windows – Outlook Express – and take advantage of the type of e-mail service typically provided by ISPs.

How does e-mail work (roughly)?

'Will I still get my messages if I'm not online when they arrive?'
'Will I still get my messages when the computer's turned off?'
'Will I still get my messages if I go on holiday?'

Yes, yes, and three times yes. To understand how e-mail works, it helps to picture a whole bunch of 'mail *servers*' connected together in the internet. A mail server is a computer responsible for storing and forwarding e-mail messages on yours and everybody else's behalf.

Let's suppose that Jack sends you an e-mail, and that your e-mail address is angus.fridge@groovyisp.com. His computer's modem sends the message through the telephone line to his ISP, where it is received by a mail server. This computer then checks the latter part of the delivery address – the bit after the @ sign – and sends the message off to another mail server somewhere on the internet en route to your ISP. Now, the message may take a convoluted and, indeed, global route, passing through many different mail servers in many geographical locations, but eventually it winds up on a mail server owned by Groovy ISP. This computer then identifies the ultimate recipient (i.e. you) from the first part of the e-mail address, and sticks it in a holding area, a little like a pigeon hole. Next time you log on to the internet and look for new messages, the server sends Jack's e-mail to your computer. If you don't check your e-mail for days at a time, that's just fine.

A couple of quick notes. Any ISP will only hold uncollected e-mail for a certain specified period – normally a few weeks, sometimes months – so don't leave it too long. Also, ISPs usually impose a size limit on e-mails, typically five or ten megabytes per message. This is understandable, as mail servers would soon fill up if required to store hundreds of Gigabytes of uncollected mail indefinitely. Furthermore, large e-mails take longer to send and receive because more data has to be transferred across the internet. You should always remember that the recipient of your messages probably has to pay telephone charges while connected to the internet, and nobody will thank you for an unasked-for 'funny' video clip that takes twenty minutes to download.

Configuring Outlook Express

Let's set up Outlook Express as your e-mail program. (Again, if you used a CD-ROM supplied by your ISP to set up your account, all of this may be pre-configured.) When you run the program for the very first time, the Internet Connection Wizard may pop right up, in which case skip to Step 2.

1

 Start

E-mail icon

Outlook Express

Set up a Mail account

There is a shortcut to Outlook Express in the pinned programs part of the Start Menu. When the program launches, click Outlook Express in the upper of the two panes on the left side. In the main window, look for an option to set up a Mail account. Click this now to launch the Internet Connection Wizard.

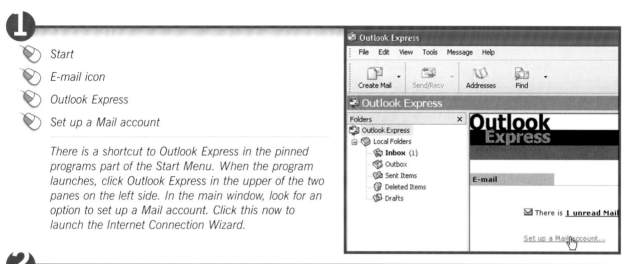

2

[your name]

Next

When somebody receives an e-mail from you, this is how you will be identified. Type in your name exactly as you wish it to appear.

3

[your e-mail address]

Next

This is the e-mail address arranged with your ISP when you first signed up. Be sure to enter it accurately. E-mail addresses are always lowercase.

4

🅣🅨🅟🅔 [incoming mail server]

🅣🅨🅟🅔 [outgoing mail server]

👆 Next

The tricky bit. Here you must enter the names of your ISP's mail servers. You can only get this information from your ISP but it would have been provided when you signed up. If not, give them a call.

5

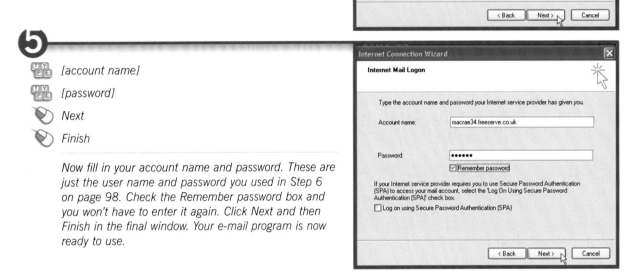

🅣🅨🅟🅔 [account name]

🅣🅨🅟🅔 [password]

👆 Next

👆 Finish

Now fill in your account name and password. These are just the user name and password you used in Step 6 on page 98. Check the Remember password box and you won't have to enter it again. Click Next and then Finish in the final window. Your e-mail program is now ready to use.

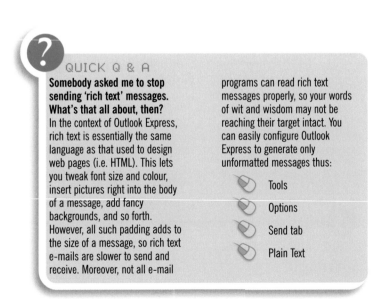

QUICK Q & A

Somebody asked me to stop sending 'rich text' messages. What's that all about, then?
In the context of Outlook Express, rich text is essentially the same language as that used to design web pages (i.e. HTML). This lets you tweak font size and colour, insert pictures right into the body of a message, add fancy backgrounds, and so forth. However, all such padding adds to the size of a message, so rich text e-mails are slower to send and receive. Moreover, not all e-mail programs can read rich text messages properly, so your words of wit and wisdom may not be reaching their target intact. You can easily configure Outlook Express to generate only unformatted messages thus:

👆 Tools

👆 Options

👆 Send tab

👆 Plain Text

E-mail basics

When you launch Outlook Express, it should look something like this. Here is a key to all the relevant features.

Title Bar *This shows you which folder is currently open within the program. Note the standard minimise window, maximise window and close program buttons at the far right.*

Menu Bar *As with Internet Explorer, click any word for a dropdown menu. The most useful of these is the Options section of the Tools menu. Here you can, for example, configure Outlook Express to automatically check for new messages every so many minutes while you're online.*

Message pane *This is where you view pertinent details about messages stored in any of the folders in the Folder pane – the 'subject' of the message, and who sent it, and when. Again, we'll see this in action shortly.*

Folders pane *Outlook Express lets you work with e-mail messages in a series of folders. Here we find:*

Inbox *Incoming messages are stored here.*

Outbox *A holding area for messages ready to be sent the next time the computer connects to the internet.*

Sent Items *Once a message has been sent, it moves from the Outbox folder to Sent Items. This gives you a record of your outgoing messages.*

Deleted Items *Much like the Windows Recycle Bin (see page 56), this folder is a holding area for messages that you have deleted. You can permanently delete messages from here by right-clicking the Deleted Items icon and selecting Empty 'Deleted Items' Folder from the pop-up menu.*

Drafts *If you save a message midway through composition, this is where it is kept. You can retrieve a draft message at any time to continue working on it.*

Toolbar *Nice big buttons that do obvious things. We'll look at these in turn when we practise working hands-on with Outlook Express.*

Contacts pane *You can store contact details here to save having to remember people's e-mail addresses. Click the arrow next to the word Contacts, then New Contact, and complete a 'card' for each contact. By default, Outlook Express automatically creates a contact card every time you reply to a message from a new correspondent. To delete a contact, highlight the entry in the Contacts pane and press the Delete key.*

Preview pane *In this window, you can read the message selected in the Message pane above. Note the scrollbar on the right for scrolling through long messages. Here we see the standard welcome message that accompanies Outlook Express (it's worth a read).*

Status bar *This tells you a little about the program's current activity.*

Sending and receiving e-mail

We will now send and receive an e-mail message. But before we start, a word about using Outlook Express on- and offline.

If your computer is already connected to the internet when you launch Outlook Express, you can check for new messages very easily by clicking the Send/Recv button on the Toolbar. You can also compose a message and send it immediately. However, if your computer is not currently connected, Outlook Express will ask whether you wish to go online now (*see below*).

The correct response rather depends upon your intentions. If you wish to check for new messages and perhaps scribble a quick reply or two, we'd suggest going online straight away. Click Yes and Outlook Express will dial up your ISP and make the connection.

If, on the other hand, you wish to compose a lengthy new e-mail, click No. Now you can work on your message at your leisure, perhaps even saving it in the Draft folder and completing it later, without having to pay telephone charges all the while.

In this example, we will begin in offline mode, so take it as read that we clicked the No button.

QUICK Q & A
How do I know that my e-mail message has been delivered?
In fact, you don't – but you will find out if it hasn't been delivered. Any message that fails to reach its destination is 'bounced' back to you by a mail server and re-appears in your Inbox with a note to that effect. By far the most common reason for non-delivery is getting somebody's e-mail address slightly wrong. There is no margin for error here. This is why it helps to use Contacts and the Address Book in Outlook Express, as you only ever have to type the address correctly once (and not even that if you reply to a message from a contact; remember, Outlook Express automatically creates contact details for your correspondents).

 Create Mail

[e-mail address]

Click the Create Mail button on the Toolbar. Up pops an e-mail window. Remember, you can easily resize this window (see page 30). The blinking cursor is already in the To: box, so type your correspondent's e-mail address here. In this case, we'd suggest that you send your first e-mail to … yourself.

[subject line]

All e-mail messages have a short subject line, which might be a simple 'Hello' or a potted summary of the message, like 'Here's that business report you asked for.' Click once in the Subject: box to move the blinking cursor, and then start typing.

[message]

Send

Now click anywhere within the main message window to move the blinking cursor into that area, and type the 'body' of your message. This is just like using WordPad (see pages 40 – 43). When you're finished, click the Send button on the e-mail window's Toolbar (not, note, the main program Toolbar).

OK

At this point, the e-mail window disappears and Outlook Express informs you that your message will be transferred to the Outbox. Click OK. If you had been online at this point, the message would be sent immediately.

Send/Recv

Yes

Click the Send/Recv button on the main program Toolbar and confirm that you wish to go online. Outlook Express now dials up your ISP and sends the message. At the same time, the program also checks for any new messages for you on your ISP's incoming mail server. If so, it retrieves them and files them in your Inbox folder.

Send/Recv

Inbox

[select message]

In this case, we fully expect delivery of our test message. Wait a minute or so and click Send/Recv again. When you see a blue figure appear next to the Inbox folder in the Folders pane – this is the number of unread messages awaiting your attention – click Inbox. Now select the test message by clicking the little closed envelope icon next to the sender's name. The body of the message will be displayed in the Preview pane.

[select message]

 Reply

 [message]

 Send

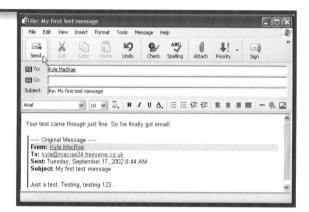

Let's now reply to this message. Select the message in the Message pane as before and click the Reply button on the main Toolbar. This opens a new e-mail window in which the recipient's name already appears in the To: box (this is actually an e-mail address in disguise). What's more, the message to which you are replying is automatically 'quoted' within the body of this new message. This helps correspondents keep track of an e-mail conversation. The blinking cursor will be blinking invitingly in the message window at this point, so type your reply message and click Send. This time, because you are already online, the message departs almost immediately (it moves to the Outbox for a few seconds first).

 Send/Recv

 Inbox

 [select message]

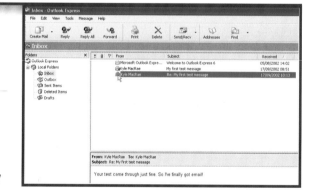

Once more, click the Send/Recv button to check for new messages, then select this latest e-mail when it arrives in the Inbox. Note that the subject line is now prefixed by 'Re:'. This is Outlook Express's way of flagging that a message is a reply to another message. You have now sent yourself an e-mail, replied to it, and received the reply. Sending and receiving e-mail to a wider audience works in exactly the same way. When you close Outlook Express, you should see the same Auto Disconnect box that popped up when closing Internet Explorer (see page 100).

Getting fancy

We have really only scratched the surface of e-mail's possibilities, so here are a few suggestions that you may care to play with.

Deleting. *To delete a message, select it in the Message pane and either press the* `Del` *key or drag it to the Deleted Items folder.*

Forwarding. *You can forward a copy of any received message to any correspondent. Select the message in the Message pane, click the Forward button on the Toolbar, and enter the recipient's e-mail address. You can add your own comments in the message window or click Send now to forward the message just as it arrived.*

Contacts. *When composing an e-mail message, click the little icon next to the To: button. This fires up the Address Book – a list of all your existing contacts. Highlight the relevant name, click the To: button and then click OK. This automatically enters the recipient's e-mail address in the e-mail window.*

Carbon copy. *If you want to send the same e-mail to two people simultaneously, enter the second e-mail address in the Cc: box. If you want to send it to multiple recipients, separate each address with a semi-colon.*

Spelling. *Outlook Express can check your spelling when you compose a message. Click Tools followed by Options and then Spelling, and check the 'Always check spelling' box.*

.

Folders. *As your Inbox fills up, create new folders in which to store older messages. Select Local Folders in the Folders pane and click File followed by Folder and then New. Give the new folder a name and click OK. It now appears in the Folder pane.*

File messages. *To file an e-mail, select it in the Message pane and drag-and-drop it on the target folder in the Folder pane. The message now moves from the Inbox to that folder. Alternatively, right-click the message, select Move to Folder from the pop-up menu, and select the target folder from the list.*

Attaching files. *You can send a copy of a file from your computer's hard disk to an e-mail correspondent. Compose a message as usual then click the Attach button in the e-mail window. Find the file on your computer, and click Attach. Remember, your ISP will impose limits on the size of files that can be e-mailed. As a guide, 500 **Kilobytes** (half of one Megabyte) is about as big as you should go unless both you and the recipient have a broadband connection and you have asked permission to send a large file.*

Viewing an attachment. *Likewise, people can send you files with e-mail. You know when you've received an attachment because (a) the message takes longer to download, and (b) a paperclip icon appears next to the message in the Message pane.*
To save the attachment, click the larger paperclip icon at the top of the Preview pane, select Save Attachments from the menu, and pick a suitable folder on your hard disk. As always, we'd suggest the My Documents folder or a sub-folder within it.
And what of viruses? Quite right. See page 120.

QUICK Q & A

How can I check how big a file is before I e-mail it?
You can check the size of any file by navigating to it with My Documents, right-clicking its icon, and selecting Properties from the pop-up menu. Its size will be expressed in bytes if it's tiny, Kilobytes if it's bigger, and Megabytes if it's a whopper.

Inserting pictures. *You can even place a picture file right into the body of an e-mail message. To do this, compose your message as usual and click Insert on the e-mail window Toolbar. Now click Picture and then use the Browse button to locate the image on your hard disk. Click Open and OK and the picture will appear in the body of the message, below any text you have typed.*

PART 4 Internet nasties

Sadly, the internet has a downside, and it's considerable. Here we touch upon a few net-borne nasties.

Viruses, and how to avoid them

Broadly speaking, a computer virus is a small software program with the potential to do damage to your computer's settings, to delete or modify your files, to allow a third party to access your hard disk without your knowledge, to replicate itself and spread from computer to computer, to do nothing of any consequence whatsoever, or any combination of the above. They go by the name of worms, script viruses, macro viruses, Trojan horses and more. They are all to be avoided.

Most viruses these days are delivered and spread by e-mail, usually in the form of a file attachment. Opening the attachment launches the virus, at which point your computer is infected and the damage is done. A particularly virulent virus can then e-mail itself to everybody in your contacts list, thereby spreading exponentially and globally.

However – and we really cannot stress this strongly enough – you can avoid viruses by taking a few simple precautions.

An antivirus program is essential protection against harmful bugs.

Live without the Preview Pane for increased security.

First and foremost, buy and install some antivirus software. Then read the manual carefully and configure the program to work at the maximum protection level. This ensures that, among other things, it automatically 'scans' e-mail attachments for viruses.

It is equally important to download regular updates from the developer's website to ensure that you're always protected against recently discovered viruses. Just about every antivirus program worth the purchase price can be easily configured to update itself automatically.

Furthermore, *never* open an e-mail attachment unless you know the sender and you are expecting the file. True, your antivirus software should detect the virus but it's always possible for a brand new virus or a previously unseen mutation to slip through the net.

For maximum safety, do away with the Preview pane in Outlook Express. Merely viewing a message can, on occasion, lead to infection. To do this, click View on the Toolbar, then Layout, and uncheck the Show Preview pane box. Now click Apply and OK.

In practice, virus hoaxes are almost as damaging as the real thing. Mark these words, one day you'll receive an e-mail that (a) graphically describes a new 'undetectable' virus that will allegedly chew up your hard disk and spit it out, and (b) exhort you to warn everybody you know without delay. Sheer nonsense, of course, but people are fooled every time. Whenever you see such a message, check it out before acting. An excellent website that sorts hoaxes from the real thing is Vmyths: www.vmyths.com.

Keep hackers at bay with a firewall.

Firewalls, and how to use them

A firewall is a software barrier that stops somebody from accessing your PC through the internet – and perhaps stealing or deleting your files –without your say-so. There are many commercial firewalls around but Windows XP also has its own firewall built in.

Back in Step 6 on page 98, when we set up an internet connection, you may have noticed that the Internet Connection Firewall option was checked. This means that your computer is automatically shielded against intrusion from hackers, which is just as it should be. Check the firewall's status at any time with this procedure:

 My Network Places icon

View network connections

[ISP] icon

Properties

Advanced

A pop-up ad pretending to be something useful. Get wise to such nonsense.

Pop-ups, and how to kill them

The world wide web is riddled with intrusive advertising. Indeed, on many websites, it's hard to find the real content amidst all the banner ads and eye-catching 'special offers'. What really drives us mad, though, are pop-ups – that is, adverts that appear in a separate window without so much as a by-your-leave. There you are, happily reading a web page, when up pops an advert for, say, a credit card. Your view is obscured and you have to close this unasked-for window before you can proceed. Some pop-ups are more persistent and just keep popping up time after time.

Worse, many adverts are disguised as computer error messages or warnings, and it's all too easy to think that Windows is trying to tell you something. It's not – somebody is trying to sell you something. Some ads even have what looks like a Close button, but this is just another trick: click the fake 'button' and you'll be taken straight to the advertiser's website.

Our advice is keep your wits about you as you surf. Close pop-ups as soon as they appear, and avoid clicking any advert unless you genuinely do want to find out more. If pop-ups become a plague, consider getting a software utility that stops them in their tracks. One such is called Pop-Up Stopper. It can be downloaded free of charge from Panicware at www.panicware.com.

Spyware, and how to sniff it out

Even worse than pop-ups are programs that worm their way into your computer, surreptitiously monitor your surfing, and report back to base. These 'spyware' programs usually masquerade as some really helpful utility, but you should never, ever install anything unless you're absolutely sure that you need and want it.

Spyware should not be confused with plug-ins, however. A plug-in is a browser enhancement that lets you view special web pages and certain multimedia effects. These are usually worth downloading and installing – in fact, the likes of Macromedia Flash Player or Apple QuickTime are essential to view some websites at all. Again, be careful and selective. Two anti-spyware programs that we use and like are Ad-aware, from LavaSoft (www.lavasoftusa.com), and SpyStopper from InfoWorks Technology Company (www.itcompany.com).

Spam, and how to live with it

Spam is unsolicited commercial e-mail, the electronic equivalent of junk mail but with one important difference: it's you who pays for it (in terms of telephone charges for your internet connection). Spam is a huge pain in the posterior.

However, you can destroy spam as quickly as it arrives in your Inbox with a single press of the Delete key. You can also, if you wish, report offending e-mails to SpamCop at http://spamcop.net (this, incidentally, is an example of a web address where you do need to include the 'http://' partly because there is no 'www' prefix. What you must never do – never, ever, ever – is reply to a spam message, especially if it has a 'click here to unsubscribe from our mailing list' option. This merely confirms that your e-mail address is 'live', and you'll be inundated with fresh spam before you can say 'delicious pork luncheon meat has no connection with unsolicited commercial bulk e-mail whatsoever.'

You can also limit the flow by keeping your e-mail address as private as possible. That is, don't use it in public *web forums* or *newsgroups* – spammers 'harvest' addresses wherever they can find them – and don't register for any product or service on the internet unless you're happy that the company won't sell, rent or otherwise disseminate your personal data for marketing purposes. Best of all, keep one e-mail address as a deliberate spam magnet, and use it in place of your primary, personal address whenever there's a risk of attracting spam. A web-based e-mail service is perfect for this.

Rid your system of sneaky spyware with this free utility.

PART 5 **Appendices**

APPENDICES

Appendix 1
System Restore

On day one, your brand new computer will 'just work'. But on day two, and day three, and forever thereafter, you run the risk of trouble. One day, inevitably, your computer either won't start at all or will start misbehaving – and come that day, you'll wish that you could roll back time and undo whatever it was that caused the trouble.

Well, you can, thanks to System Restore – a rescue routine for your computer.

Good practice

System Restore works by taking regular 'snapshots' (called restore points) of your computer's most important settings. Should something go awry, you have the opportunity to revert to an earlier restore point and, hopefully, recover from the problem.

System Restore works in the background and really needs very little thought or intervention. It creates restore points automatically whenever you install a Windows Update (p.128) or install a new program. However, it doesn't hurt to occasionally make restore points manually, particularly just before (not after!) making any significant change to your computer, such as plugging in a new piece of hardware. Also, because Windows doesn't *always* recognise new program installations, we'd strongly recommend that you make a manual restore point before loading any new software. Here's how …

Making and restoring a restore point

Start

All Programs

Accessories

System Tools

System Restore

Create a restore point

Next

Close all programs, return to the Desktop and follow these directions to launch System Restore. Check Create a restore point and then click the Next button.

 [checkpoint name]

Create

Close

Give the restore point a meaningful name (i.e. one that you can identify later, if need be) and click the Create button. Windows then takes its snapshot of your system and confirms when its finished. Click Close on the next window. That's it.

③

👆 *Start*

👆 *All Programs*

👆 *Accessories*

👆 *System Tools*

👆 *System Restore*

👆 *Restore my computer to an earlier time*

👆 *Next*

👆 *Select restore point*

👆 *Next*

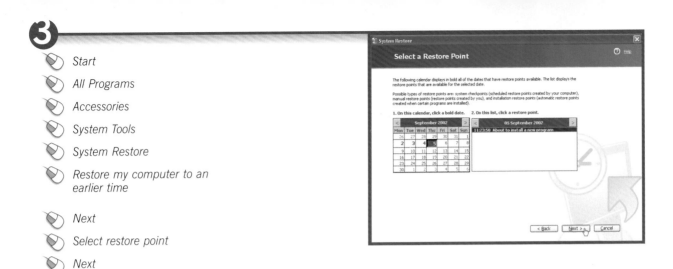

Let's now suppose that you have a hiccup and need to revert to your last restore point.
Launch System Restore as above but this time select the Restore option. In the next window, a calendar appears, and you can click on any day to see a list of possible restore points. However, the computer's most recent point is displayed by default – in this case, the one we just made. Select it and click Next.

④

👆 *Next*

👆 *OK*

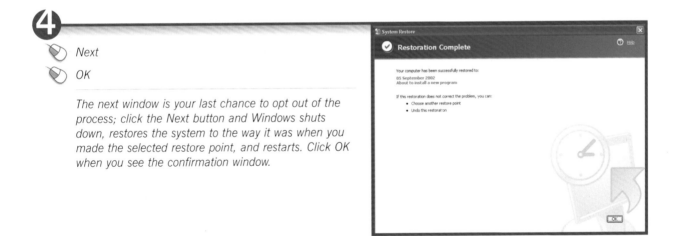

The next window is your last chance to opt out of the process; click the Next button and Windows shuts down, restores the system to the way it was when you made the selected restore point, and restarts. Click OK when you see the confirmation window.

Life saver

Now, if this solves the problem with your computer, great. Otherwise, you can either undo the restoration – you'll see an option to do just that if you run System Restore again – or restore your computer to an even earlier time.

Incidentally, System Restore works entirely at a deep-rooted level and does not affect your own files and folders, so don't worry that you'll lose today's work if you roll back to yesterday's restore point.

In rare circumstances, Windows may be unable to start your computer normally. Should this happen, System Restore will kick in before Windows starts. Pick the most recent restore point and see if that gets Windows working; otherwise, keep trying earlier points.

PART **5**

Appendix 2
Keep Windows current

From time to time, you're bound to hear a news item proclaiming that (yet another) security vulnerability has been discovered in Windows and several million people's computers are now at risk from hackers. In such cases, there's usually a postscript to the effect that Microsoft has a 'patch' available for download. But what on earth are they talking about?

Fixing a hole

Patches are just what they sound like – software sticking-plasters that keep Windows up to date. A patch is a bit of computer code that integrates with the rest of Windows and plugs a hole or adds a little new functionality. Some patches are 'critical', others are 'recommended' but none are actually obligatory. Moreover, once or twice within the lifecycle of a major product like Windows XP Home Edition, Microsoft releases a whopping patch called a 'Service Pack' that addresses a whole host of issues in one fell swoop.

Having to download regular patches is undeniably a bit of a pain and some would argue that it really shouldn't be necessary. However, patches and Service Packs are free and usually make your computer (a) more secure and (b) better in some small way. We would advise that you download and install all 'critical' patches and Service Packs as they become available, and exercise your own judgement over whether you need any of the optional bells and whistles.

Manual updates

You can look for patches and updates at any time by visiting Microsoft's Windows Updates website. In fact, there's a shortcut in your Start Menu: click

 Start

 All Programs

 Windows Update.

This launches Internet Explorer and takes you straight to the relevant web page.

On your first visit, you'll be prompted to download a small program. Click the Yes button. In a minute or two, the page will display a link called Scan for updates. Click this now.

The downloaded program now scans your version of Windows, checks to see which if any patches have already been installed, and reports its findings back to the Windows Update website. It takes a few minutes but eventually you'll see a list of all available lists in the left-hand window pane. Click any category to expand the list in the right-hand pane. Now decide which updates you want, add each in turn to your download list by clicking the Add button beside it, and then click the Review and install updates link to start the download.

Be sure to follow the instructions closely, and confirm that you have read and accept the licensing terms when prompted. You will probably have to restart your computer when the download is complete.

On your next visit, you can skip the initial program download. But it's still a bit of a faff, isn't it? And it relies upon you remembering to check for updates. Let's make life a little easier …

Automatic updates

Periodically, Windows sends a balloon to the Notification Area of the Taskbar, inviting you to configure automatic updates. Click this balloon to launch the Automatic Updates Setup Wizard.

This is simplicity itself – click Next and check the option that lets Windows download patches on the fly whenever you happen to be connected to the internet, and then asks your permission to install them at a convenient time. This means that you never need give patches or security holes a second thought.

APPENDICES

Appendix 3
User accounts

Windows is customisable in all manner of ways, from the background picture on your Desktop to the colours used on screen and the way files and folders are displayed. With user accounts, it's even possible to set up a single computer to look and behave quite differently depending upon who's using it at the time. Stuffy dad may want a business-orientated machine with a minimum of frills and distractions; teenage son may prefer a Britney background and a focus on high-speed internet gaming; studious daughter may wish to ensure that her research files are not accidentally deleted by her careless brother (and perhaps keep him away from her private diary). User accounts let each member of the family arrange things entirely to their own suiting without affecting how others use the computer. What's more, each user account is protected with a password so the kids can't muck up dad's settings (and, to some extent, vice versa).

One for all the family

There are two levels of user accounts: *Administrator*, where the user can make system-wide changes, including installing and uninstalling programs; and *Limited*, where the user can make changes to his or her own account but not interfere with the computer's main settings. We'll assume in the following example that you are the administrator. Let's now set up a limited account for Jack, your son.

Start

Control Panel

User Accounts icon

Owner icon

First, you need to set up your own account. Click Owner to open a window where you can make changes to the account. As the sole user of the computer, you automatically have an Administrator account.

Change my name

 [your name]

 Change name

Type in your name or the title by which you wish to be identified (Mum, Dad or whatever).

 Create a password

 [password]

 [password]

 [password hint]

 8 Create password

Here you set up an access password and leave yourself a hint in case you ever forget it. This password will let you access your own settings, files and folders on the computer – and keep everybody else out. Click once in each box to move the blinking cursor there before you start typing.

 Yes, Make Private

Click this option to ensure that Jack cannot view, edit or delete your files and folders.

 Create a new account

Back at the User Accounts window, you might care to change your picture (this appears at the top of the Start Menu) but we'll skip straight to setting up an account for Jack. The new account option is in Related Tasks pane on the left.

131

Jack

 Next

Limited

Create Account

In the next window, type in the account name: Jack, in
this example. In the following window, check the
Limited account option and then click Create Account.

 Jack icon

You are now back at main User Account window. Click
the icon for Jack's account and, as in Step 3 above,
give Jack his own password – or, if you trust him, leave
the room and let him set his own password and
password hint.

 Choose the way users log on or off

 Apply Options

Back at the main window again, click the logging on
configuration option and ensure that both options are
checked (they should be by default). Now close the
User Accounts window and leave Control Panel.

 Start

 Log Off

 Switch User

Let's see it in action. Click Log Off in the Start Menu
followed by Switch User. Now Jack can log in to his
account and set up Windows to his own liking without
affecting your settings. You don't even have to close any
programs you have running when switching accounts –
they will still be running when you return. This is
obviously a whole lot easier than turning your computer
off and back on again.

Jack icon

 [password] Enter

Jack simply clicks his icon, types in his password and presses the Enter key to access his account. To return to your account, repeat Step 9 from within Jack's account and click your own icon. Also, whenever you or Jack turns the computer off, the first thing you'll see when you turn it back on again is a Windows welcome screen that lets you choose who should log on first.

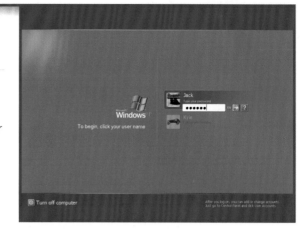

Points to note

Because you selected the privacy option in Step 4, Jack cannot see any of your files. However, Windows has a Shared Documents folder for the express purpose of letting you share certain files. Any file in here can be accessed by all account holders regardless of whether they have Administrator or Limited account status. You'll find the Shared Documents in the Other Places part of the My Documents window.

Furthermore, because you have an Administrator account, you can see all Jack's files (although it's not immediately obvious how). Follow this procedure:

 My Computer icon

 C: icon

 Documents and Settings icon

 Jack icon

 Jack's Documents icon

It takes a lot of double-clicking but eventually you arrive at Jack's own My Documents folder. This is quite distinct from yours.

Now that Jack and you have separate accounts, you each can arrange your Desktop, files, folders and personal settings however you like. Chances are that Jack's computer (so to speak) will end up looking remarkably different from your own. We're not going to look at how to customise Windows any further in this manual – it's hardly an essential part of home computing – but take it from us that Jack will know just what to do.

PART # Appendix 4
Trouble-shooting

We have already covered different ways to keep Windows running smoothly, notably by installing updates and making well-timed restore points. However, should all go pear-shaped, there is plenty more you can do. Here we consider a couple of options.

Help and Support Center

Windows can attempt to find and resolve hardware or software problems automatically, which is ideal if the internal machinations of your system are something of a mystery.

Start

Help and Support

Use Tools to view your computer information and diagnose problems.

Pretty obvious so far.

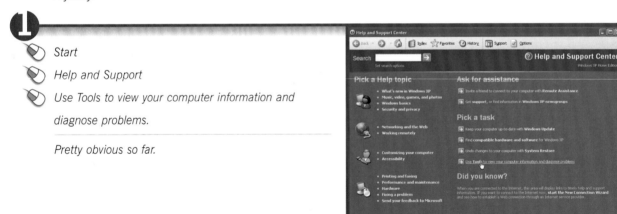

My Computer Information

View the status of my system hardware and software

When you make this choice, Windows analyses the current condition of your computer.

[appropriate option]

After a minute or two, you'll see a report like this, broken down into sections. At this point, you can click the Trouble-shooter option next to whichever area is causing concern. If, for instance, your computer refuses to play any sounds, click the Sound Card Trouble-shooter; or if the monitor starts displaying weird colours, click the Video Card option.

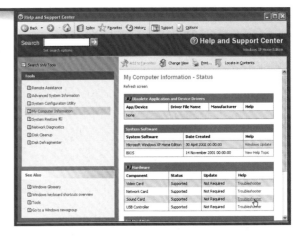

[appropriate responses]

What follows is a question-and-answer session. It can get a little confusing but take your time and read the messages carefully. Results are not guaranteed, unfortunately, but Windows will have a pretty good bash at resolving the problem.

Alternatively, you can type keywords into the Help and Support Center's internal search engine. This should take you directly to relevant information.

Note the link at the bottom of the left pane to something called the Microsoft Knowledge Base. This is a truly massive repository of helpful information on the web that goes well beyond the scope of the Help topics built into Windows itself. To access the Knowledge Base, search for help on your keywords as above *while your computer is online*, and then click the link. Now you can select articles in the left pane and read them in full in the right pane. Bear in mind that this does rather presuppose that you have a working internet connection!

The Knowledge Base has been compiled over many years and it covers all versions of Windows, so include the term 'XP' in your keywords to increase relevancy. It also tends to get very technical at times, so take a deep breath before wading in.

Newsgroups

Still no luck? Well, again assuming that you can get your computer online, you could try asking fellow computer owners for help. Newsgroups are discussion groups in which people exchange messages (often in rather robust language and with a fair degree of attitude, it has to be said), and there are plenty devoted to Windows, hardware and software issues. You can browse existing discussions to see if your particular problem is discussed, or you can post your own request for assistance and wait for a response (it may not be immediate, but you will get one).

You can access the Windows XP-specific newsgroups in two ways. The short route is by launching Internet Explorer and going straight to the following web page:

www.microsoft.com/windowsxp/expertzone/newsgroups/default.asp

Alternatively, do this:

 Start

 Help and Support

 Get support, or find information in Windows XP newsgroups

 Go to a Windows Web site forum

 Go to Windows Newsgroups

This will launch Internet Explorer and find the relevant page.

Once there, take the time to read the 'Frequently Asked Questions' section and the bit on 'How to Participate'.

Above all, remember to back up your important files regularly, as discussed on page 76. Even in the worst eventuality, you need never lose your work.

Glossary

PART **5**

Here we explain some of the terms mentioned but not really explored in the main part of the manual.

4.1/5.1 When an audio signal is split into several discrete channels and played back over correctly positioned speakers, the listener feels literally surrounded by sound (hence the term surround sound). A 4.1 speaker system uses four satellite speakers (two stereo speakers to the front and two behind) plus a subwoofer. In a 5.1 system, there is an additional central channel/speaker devoted to spoken dialogue in movie soundtracks.

Always-on In the context of broadband, a fixed internet connection that does not rely upon a modem dialling an ISP over a telephone line. You can leave an always-on connection active around the clock without racking up telephone charges.

A 4.1 speaker set up for surround sound.

Analogue A signal that varies continuously over time. For example, when a person speaks, the sound wave is an analogue signal, varying smoothly as they talk. Think of the hands on a traditional clock.

Background A program that works in the background is not obvious to the user (i.e. it doesn't appear in a window).

Bad old days Before Windows came DOS, a text-based operating system for personal computers. DOS is a mystery to most of us. Praise be for that.

Binary data A computer stores information in a coded form that involves nothing but long strings of 1s and 0s (i.e. it uses the binary numbering system).

Bit The smallest chunk of computer code, or data, consisting of a single 1 or 0.

Examples of buttons

Broken In the context of the web, a broken page has a problem which prevents it from being displayed properly in the browser. This could be a fault with the way the page has been coded or a blip with the server on which it is held.

Button An element of a program designed to look like a button. You can point at and click buttons with the mouse, at which point something will happen.

Cable Broadband internet access is often available through the same fibre-optic cables used to bring television and telephone services to homes and businesses.

A recordable CD drive gives you better backup options – and makes audio CDs to boot.

CD burning The process of saving files to a compact disc. Commercial CDs are pressed, much like vinyl records of old, but a computer drive uses a laser to burn a pattern onto the surface of the disc.

CD-R CD-Recordable. Recordable CDs can be filled with files once and once only.

CD-ROM CD-Read-Only Memory. Files can be read *from* a CD-ROM disc but you cannot record, or save, files to the disc.

CD-RW CD-ReWriteable. Rewriteable CDs can be filled with files repeatedly. Old files can be deleted to make space for new ones.

Check To check an option is to turn a particular feature on. To uncheck it is to turn that feature off.

Copy To copy a file is to create an exact digital duplicate of it without in any way affecting the original file.

CRT Cathode Ray Tube. A glass tube used to produce an image on some television sets and some computer monitors.

A CRT monitor.

Data Any bit or collection of information used by or stored on a computer.

Default In the context of computing, a default option is selected automatically. For instance, a printer might print in draft mode b default. The use of 'default' implies that an alternative is available.

Delete To delete a file is to remove all record of it from a hard disk or other storage media. In practice, deleted files are not physically removed until some fresh file is allocated to the same disk space. This is why deleted files can often be 'magically' recovered.

Diagnostic utility A program that attempts to find and resolve problems with your computer.

Dialogue box A window used by Windows to proffer information, offer choices and invite responses.

Dial-up An internet connection that relies upon a modem making a successful data call to an ISP over a telephone line.

Digital In contrast to analogue, a digital signal is composed of discrete packets of information (i.e. it moves sharply between fixed values. In terms of data, the digital data that your computer works with is 'simply' a string of 1s and 0s).

An external modem.

Disc/disk Disc is used with reference to *optical* storage media, such as a compact disc, and disk with reference to *magnetic* media, as in a floppy or hard disk.

Domain The top-level name of a website.

Download To download something is to transfer a copy of it from one computer to your own, especially but not exclusively across the internet.

Drive activity light A warning light that illuminates when a drive is busy working with data. The system unit has such a light, as do most CD/DVD drives. You should never remove a floppy disk while the light is on.

DSL Digital Subscriber Line. A technology that converts an ordinary household telephone line into a broadband internet connection. ADSL is most common version in the UK (the A stands for Asymmetric), with which you can download data faster than you can upload it (hence the asymmetry).

DVD movie A movie distributed on a DVD disc, as opposed to, for instance, a video cassette. A DVD drive with the right software, video card and sound card can play DVD movies on a computer.

DVD-ROM Just like CD-ROM, this is a 'read only' medium. DVD discs look just like compact discs but can hold much more data.

DVI Digital Visual Interface. A standard used to connect digital monitors to computers. A digital monitor can broadcast the pure digital signal generated by the computer's video card, with a resultant improvement in quality over that of analogue monitors, where the signal must first be converted from digital to analogue.

Don't forget to install a software player if you want to watch movies on your computer.

Ethernet A high-speed standard used to connect computers with cables in a network.

File-sharing In the context of the internet, file-sharing involves making selected files on your computer available to other people, usually anonymously. File-sharing gained notoriety when it proved an immensely popular way of swapping pirated material, particularly music.

Gigabyte A measure of data size. One Gigabyte is 1,024 Megabytes.

Hacker Somebody with the ability or aspiration to break into your computer through the internet, illegally.

Help menu In the context of a program, this is a (usually) searchable index of common questions and answers. If you get stuck, look for a Help button on the program Toolbar.

Hit In the context of search engines, a hit is a web page that contains some or all of your keywords.

Hyperlink An element on a web page that, if clicked, opens another web page in your browser.

Icon A small image used by Windows to identify a file or program.

Instant chat/

instant messenger An instant messenger program lets you conduct real-time two-way text conversations (called chat) across the internet. Windows comes with its own instant messenger – look in All Programs for Windows Messenger.

Interface In the context of software, the 'look and feel' of a program, such as its buttons, menus and windows. In hardware terms, it usually refers to a physical connection, like the USB interface.

Kilobyte A measure of data size. One Kilobyte is 1024 bytes (and one byte is 8 bits).

LCD Liquid Crystal Display. A technology used to create flat-screen monitors that are much slimmer and lighter than CRT monitors.

There's no getting away from it: LCD monitors are infinitely sleeker and sexier than their CRT cousins.

Megabyte A measure of data size. One Megabyte is 1,024 Kilobytes.

Memory Memory is used to describe physical storage areas in a computer (i.e. places where data is saved). This includes Random Access Memory (RAM), which a computer uses as a temporary storage area. While you work on a letter with a word processor program, for example, the letter is 'held in RAM', and will be lost if the computer is turned off. If you save that letter, however, the file is allocated a chunk of hard disk space – another type of memory – and can be retrieved at any time.

A RAM module.

Menu In the context of computers, a list of options from which you make a selection.

MIDI Musical Instrument Digital Interface. A standard for controlling and playing electronic musical instruments with a computer.

Modem A device that allows two computers to communicate with each other over a telephone line.

Motherboard The main circuit board inside a computer. Every other component connects to and communicates through the motherboard.

Multimedia A combination of text, sound, pictures and video.

Network Any two or more computers connected together equals a network. They can be connected with cables, wirelessly, directly, or remotely. The internet is, of course, the grand-daddy of networks.

Newsgroups Discussion groups on the internet where you can post messages, read replies from other people, and exchange files. Outlook Express can be set up to access newsgroups but you should first check whether your ISP provides access to this part of the internet (which is known as Usenet).

Online gaming You can play computer games against strangers over the internet. A broadband connection helps enormously.

Online shopping You can buy stuff from virtual shops, like Amazon.com, over the internet. You can even have your groceries delivered to your door.

Overtype To overtype is to replace old text with new text without deleting the old text first. You can generally do this when the old text is highlighted.

Parallel port A single socket on the back of a computer typically used to connect a printer (before USB took over).

Parental controls Any software measure that lets somebody control, limit, supervise or otherwise modify the way somebody else uses a computer, particularly with regard to the internet.

Plug-and-play A standard that enables a computer running Windows to automatically recognise and configure a new hardware device.

Plug it in and play straight away.

Pop-up A menu that just 'pops up' on screen.

Processor A silicon chip that processes data very, very quickly. Effectively, the brain of your computer.

Product Activation Certain Microsoft programs, including Windows XP, must be activated to keep them working beyond a certain cut-off period. This anti-piracy measure essentially involves sending a code to Microsoft (anonymously) that ties the software to your particular computer and prevents you or anybody else from installing it on multiple computers. It's controversial, but the process itself is very straightforward, particularly if you have an internet connection.

Restart To restart a computer is to turn it off and on again immediately.

Satellite Broadband internet access is available through a similar kind of satellite service that brings television to the home. It's worth considering if you can't otherwise get DSL or cable broadband, but still very expensive.

Secure In terms of the internet, a secure website is one where confidential information, such as your credit card number, is encrypted at the point of sending. Basically, it means it's safe to shop.

Select To select something is, generally speaking, to click it. Once selected, an object becomes active (i.e. the focus of current activity).

Serial A pair (usually) of ports on the back of a computer once used to connect devices like mice and modems, but now increasingly obsolete.

Serial ports

Server A computer that is linked, directly or indirectly, to other computers and can be accessed by them. Servers are commonly used for large-scale data storage. The web consists of thousands of servers on which web pages are stored.

Session In computer-speak, a session is a period spent doing something or other. An internet session is a period spent online, for example.

Sound card An expansion card that lets a computer make sounds (providing there are speakers attached), particularly useful for playing music and games.

Streaming Streaming sound and video files are downloaded to your computer piece by piece. This means that you can start listening or watching them without having to wait for the whole file to download first.

A sound card.

Subwoofer A speaker designed to broadcast very low-frequencies. An integral part of a surround sound system.

Surfing To surf is to visit web pages and click on links.

Surround sound See 4.1/5.1.

A scanner.

t

Technical support Virtually all ISPs offer some form of technical support by telephone by which you can call them up to seek assistance. This is often charged at premium rates, however. In many cases, you'll find that the ISP's customers are only too happy to pool resources and offer advice for free, often in newsgroups (see the entry above).

TWAIN A standard that get scanners talking to and working with programs. It's not an acronym, unfortunately, although urban legend insists it was coined for Technology Without An Interesting Name (we're happy to keep the myth alive).

u

USB Universal Serial Bus. A fast interface with which peripherals can connect to a computer. The beauty of USB is that it's hot-swappable, which means you can unplug one device and plug in another without restarting Windows. Now in its second, much faster incarnation, called USB 2.0.

User licence The terms and conditions governing ownership and use of a software program. Read a user licence once, just for kicks.

USB connectors.

v

VGA Video Graphics Array. The most basic standard governing a video card's output and a monitor's display capability. Also used to describe the hardware connection between the card and monitor.

Video card An expansion card that lets a computer generate images on a monitor.

w

Web forums Discussion groups contained within websites. All you need to take part is a browser.

Web page A document stored on an internet server that can be viewed by anyone with an internet connection and a browser.

Web space A chunk of reserved hard disk space on an internet server whereon you can design a web page or site. Most ISPs give you a few Megabytes of web space for free, which is ample to build a sizeable website.

Web-based e-mail An e-mail service where you send and collect messages through your browser. Because web-based e-mail is independent of ISPs (i.e. it doesn't matter how you happen to be connected to the internet at the time) it is ideal for sending and picking up messages from anywhere in the world, particularly when travelling.

z

Zipping Compressing a file to reduce the space it takes up.

Index

proprietary/non-proprietary file
  formats 89

QuickTime, Apple 123

ReadMe files 90
recovering files 68
Recycle Bin 56, 57, 68
  emptying 77
reference programs 91
Refresh, browser basics 103
renaming folders 64, 77
repeating keyboard characters
  44–5
reset switch 12
resolution, monitors 60
restarting 141
restoring
  files/folders 68
  System Restore 126–7
'rich text' e-mail messages 112
right-click, mouse 30, 39
RSI (Repetitive Strain Injury)
  17
Run 59

satellite broadband 95, 141
satellite speakers 20–1
Save As 65, 89
saving files 65–7, 89
scanners 13
  connecting 52–3
  TWAIN 52–3, 141
  USB ports 53
screen examples 8, 9
script viruses 120–3
Scrollbar 60–1
search engines 107
Searching, browser basics
  103, 107
searching for files 59, 69
secure websites 101, 141
Sent Items, e-mail 113
serial ports 14, 15, 141

servers 141
servers, mail 110, 112
Service Packs 128–9
Shortcuts 59
shortcuts, files/folders 70
single-click, mouse 61
size checking files 119
software 15
  drivers 15, 46, 48–9
  patches 128–9
  see also programs
Solitaire card game 31–3
sound cards 14, 15, 141
sound editing programs 91
spam 123
SpamCop 123
speakers 12, 13
  connections 21–2, 23
  satellite 20–1
  subwoofers 20, 22, 141
speech recognition 36, 91
Spelling check, e-mail 118
spreadsheets 91
SpyStopper 123
spyware 122–3
start button 24–5, 29
Start Menu 58–9
Status Bar 101, 113
Stop, browser basics 103
streaming 141
subwoofers 20, 22, 141
support
  Help and Support Center
    59, 134–5
  internet technical 95, 141
  newsgroups 136
surge protection 16
System Restore 126–7
system units 12
system utility programs 91

Task Manager 88
taskbar 56–7
  balloons 59
tea, making 109
technical support *see* support
telephone line sockets 14, 16
text instructions 8, 9
tiling windows 61
Title Bar 60–1, 101, 113

Toolbar 60–1, 101, 113
Tools, browser basics 102
tower system units 12, 14
Trojan horses 120–3
trouble-shooting 134–6
turning on/off 24–5, 59
TWAIN (Technology Without
  An Interesting Name),
  scanners 52–3, 141

unfreezing computers 88
uninstalling programs 86–7
uninterruptible power supply
  16
unlimited/limited access,
  internet 95
updating Windows 128–9
USB (Universal Serial Bus)
  141–2
  ports 14, 15
  printers 46, 47
  scanners 53
User accounts 130–3
user licences *see* licences, user

VGA (Video Graphics Array)
  142
video cards 15, 142
video editing programs 91
View, browser basics 102
Viewing e-mail attachments
  119
viewing files 70–1
viruses 120–3
  antivirus programs 91,
    120–1
Vmyths 121

web-based e-mail 142
web browsers *see* browsing the
  web
web editing programs 91
web forums 123, 142
web pages 142

bookmarks 105–6
broken 137
downloading 100
hits 139
opening 104–5
web space 94, 142
websites
  defined 100
  secure 101, 141
Winamp 108–9
Windows, customising 24, 34,
  130–3
Windows Update 126, 128–9
Windows XP 15, 55–91
  key concepts 56–61
word processor programs 91
WordPad 40–3, 65–7
workstations, preparing 16–17
worms 120–3
www (World Wide Web) 101

zipping files/folders 76–7, 142

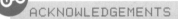

ACKNOWLEDGEMENTS

Author	**Kyle MacRae**
Project Manager	**Louise McIntyre**
Design	**Simon Larkin**
Copy editor	**John Hardaker**
Page build	**James Robertson**
Photography	**Tom Bain**
Cover photography	**Simon Clay**
Illustrations	**Matthew Marke**
Index	**Nigel d'Auvergne**
Front cover hand model	**Thomas Rendle**

The author and publisher would like to thank the following companies
for supplying products used during the preparation of this manual:

Company	Products featured	Contact
Canon	S520 Bubble Jet printer (p. 46-51	www.canon.co.uk
Mesh computers	Mesh Matrix XP 2000	www.meshcomputers.com
	+ PC system used throughout	
	(thanks, Nick)	
Microsoft	Windows XP Home Edition (passim)	www.microsoft.com/uk
Posture Point	Status Fluid chair (p. 17)	www.posture.co.uk